T0329215

Q. HORATI FLACCI

CARMINUM LIBER IV

CARMEN SAECULARE

Q. HORATI FLACCI
CARMINUM LIBER IV

WITH INTRODUCTION AND NOTES

BY

JAMES GOW

CAMBRIDGE:
AT THE UNIVERSITY PRESS
1955

CAMBRIDGE UNIVERSITY PRESS
Cambridge, New York, Melbourne, Madrid, Cape Town,
Singapore, São Paulo, Delhi, Mexico City

Cambridge University Press
The Edinburgh Building, Cambridge CB2 8RU, UK

Published in the United States of America by Cambridge University Press, New York

www.cambridge.org
Information on this title: www.cambridge.org/9781107693616

© Cambridge University Press 1896

First published 1896
First Edition 1896
Reprinted 1913, 1936, 1955
First paperback edition 2013

A catalogue record for this publication is available from the British Library

ISBN 978-1-107-69361-6 Paperback

PREFACE.

THIS edition of Horace's Odes and Epodes was undertaken at the request of the Syndics of the Pitt Press.

In the text, at a few notorious passages, I have admitted conjectures which give a good sense with very little alteration of the letters. The spelling is, for obvious reasons, adapted in the main to that of Lewis and Short's lexicon. In regard to final -*es* and -*is* in acc. plur. of the 3rd declension I have almost always followed the indications given in Keller's *Epilegomena*.

In preparing the notes, I have used Orelli's edition (as revised in 1885 by Hirschfelder) freely for illustrative quotations. It is the common quarry. Besides this, I have referred very often to the editions of A. Kiessling (1884) and Dean Wickham (1874), less frequently to those of Mr Page (1886), C. W. Nauck (1880) and H. Schütz (1874). The dates given are the dates of my copies.

I am greatly indebted to my friend Dr Postgate, of Trinity College, for many corrections and suggestions.

J. G.

NOTTINGHAM,
October, 1895.

CONTENTS.

INTRODUCTION.

§ 1. *Life of Horace.*

OUR knowledge of the life of Horace is derived chiefly from his own works, which teem with allusions to his past history and present occupations. A few minor details are supplied either by the scholiasts or by a brief biography of the poet which is found in some MSS. and which may be attributed with certainty to Suetonius (C. Suetonius Tranquillus, flor. A.D. 150).

Quintus Horatius Flaccus[1] was born on the 8th of December[2] B.C. 65[3] at Venusia, an ancient military colony situated near Mt. Voltur and the river Aufidus, on the confines of Apulia and Lucania[4].

Horace's father was a freedman, possibly a Greek by birth[5].

---

[1] For the full name cf. *Sat.* II. 6. 37, *Carm.* IV. 6. 44, *Epod.* 15. 12.

[2] For the month cf. *Epist.* I. 20. 27. The day is supplied by Suetonius.

[3] Horace names the year by the consul L. Manlius Torquatus, *Carm.* III. 21. 1 (*nata mecum consule Manlio*) and *Epod.* 13. 6.

[4] For Mt. Voltur, see *Carm.* III. 4. 10. For the rest, *Carm.* IV. 9. 2 (*longe sonantem natus ad Aufidum*), *Sat.* II. 1. 34, 35 (*Lucanus an Appulus anceps* | *nam Venusinus arat finem sub utrumque colonus*), and *Sat.* I. 6. 73 (where the Venusian boys are said to be *magnis e centurionibus orti*).

[5] *Sat.* I. 6. 6 (*me libertino patre natum*). The foundation for the suggestion that the father was a Greek is merely (1) that he had been a

By profession, he was a tax-collector or debt-collector[1], perhaps also a dealer in salt-fish (*salsamentarius*), if Suetonius may be trusted. From small beginnings[2], he seems to have acquired some fortune, sufficient, at any rate, to warrant him in removing from Venusia to Rome, and devoting himself to his son's education[3]. To his father's fond and judicious care of him, during his school days, Horace more than once bears eloquent testimony[4].

At Rome, Horace was put to an expensive school[5], kept by a crusty old grammarian, L. Orbilius Pupillus, nicknamed 'the flogger.' Here he studied, among other things, the early Latin poets[6] (such as Livius Andronicus) and the *Iliad* of Homer[7].

From school Horace proceeded (about the age of 19, no doubt) to the university of Athens, where he attended the lectures of the Academy[8]. The course would include geometry, logic, moral philosophy and probably also rhetoric or literary criticism. In after years, Horace no longer adhered to the

slave and must have been a foreigner, and (2) that Horace at an early age was sufficiently fluent in Greek to write Greek verses (*Sat.* I. 10. 31—35). It is not known how the father acquired the name of Horatius. According to usage, Flaccus ('flap-eared') would have been his slave-name and Horatius the name of his former master. (See Dict. of Antiq. 3rd ed. s. v. *Nomen.*) The colony of Venusia was enrolled in the *tribus Horatia*, and the father may have been a slave in the service of the town.

    [1] *Sat.* I. 6. 86 (*ut fuit ipse, coactor*).

    [2] *Sat.* I. 6. 71 (*macro pauper agello*).

    [3] *Sat.* I. 6. 71—96, esp. 81, 82 (*ipse mihi custos incorruptissimus omnes | circum doctores aderat*).

    [4] Besides *Sat.* I. 6, see also *Sat.* I. 4. 105 sqq.

    [5] *Sat.* I. 6. 76—80.

    [6] *Epist.* II. 1. 69—71 (*non equidem insector delendave carmina Livi | esse reor, memini quae plagosum mihi parvo | Orbilium dictare*).

    [7] *Epist.* II. 2. 41, 42 (*Romae nutriri mihi contigit atque doceri | iratus Grais quantum nocuisset Achilles*).

    [8] *Epist.* II. 2. 44, 45 (*adiecere bonae paullo plus artis Athenae, | scilicet ut vellem curvo dinoscere rectum | atque inter silvas Academi quaerere verum*).

Academic opinions in moral philosophy, but professed himself a free thinker inclined to Epicureanism[1].

During his stay at Athens, Horace made the acquaintance of many young Romans of noble birth[2], by whom apparently he was introduced, in September B.C. 44, to M. Junius Brutus[3], the Liberator. Brutus, at this time, was passing through Athens on his way to the province of Macedonia which had been assigned to him (as propraetor) by Julius Caesar before his murder. (Cassius meanwhile was proceeding to his province, Syria.) As governor of Macedonia, Brutus was collecting an army, partly to oppose C. Antonius, who claimed the province as nominee of the senate, and partly to combat some turbulent tribes of Thracians, who were harassing the borders. In this army, Horace received the appointment of military tribune[4]. He marched with the troops through Macedonia and Thrace, crossed the Hellespont, saw a good deal of Asia Minor[5] and returned with the combined forces of Brutus and Cassius to the field of Philippi (Nov. B.C. 42). In the first battle at this place, Brutus was victorious; in the second (twenty days later) he was defeated, and Horace fled[6], never to bear arms again.

[1] *Epist.* I. I. 14 (*nullius addictus iurare in verba magistri*), and *Epist.* I. 4. 16 (*Epicuri de grege porcum*). Cf. also *Carm.* I. 34. 1—5.

[2] Some of them are named in *Sat.* I. 10. 81—87.

[3] Plutarch, *Brutus*, 24.

[4] *Sat.* I. 6. 48 (*quod mihi pareret legio Romana tribuno*). The statement here is doubtless an exaggeration, for there should have been six tribunes to the legion.

[5] It is clear that Horace was at Clazomenae and saw the trial described in *Sat.* I. 7. The rest of his campaigning, before Philippi, is mere matter of inference. He speaks of Thrace in winter (e.g. *Carm.* I. 37. 20) and of the Hellespont (*Epist.* I. 3. 4) as if he had seen them, and he addresses a friend (*Carm.* II. 7. 1, 2) as ' *O saepe mecum tempus in ultimum | deducte Bruto militiae duce.*'

[6] *Carm.* II. 7. 9, 10 (*tecum Philippos et celerem fugam | sensi, relicta non bene parmula*). Cf. also *Carm.* III. 4. 26. In *Epod.* I. 16 (written ten years later than Philippi) he describes himself as *imbellis ac firmus parum.*

Soon after the battle, Horace appears to have obtained a pardon from Octavianus and leave to return to Rome. He seems to have travelled nearly all the way by sea and suffered shipwreck, or came near it, at Mons Palinurus on the Lucanian coast[1]. His father was by this time dead, and when he reached Rome, he found himself penniless[2]. It is said that he managed to procure a situation as clerk in some department of the public treasury[3] and that he held this office for about four years (B.C. 41—37). Horace himself says that poverty drove him to making verses[2], but it is unlikely that he found poetry a source of income. More probably he had introductions to some conservative (i.e. republican) coteries, and used his literary talents to make himself welcome, in spite of his poverty. No other society would have received with favour, at that time, such denunciations of civil war as Epodes 7 and 16, two of Horace's earliest pieces.

The compositions of Horace at this period were undoubtedly either satires in the manner of Lucilius (died B.C. 103), or iambic epodes, mostly satirical, in the manner of Archilochus of Paros[4] (flor. B.C. 700). Through these, probably, he obtained the acquaintance of L. Varius and Vergil, who became his fast friends and introduced him to Maecenas[5]. Some nine months

---

[1] *Carm.* III. 4. 28 and 27. 18.

[2] *Epist.* II. 2. 49—52. (*unde simul primum me dimisere Philippi,* | *decisis humilem pennis inopemque paterni* | *et laris et fundi paupertas impulit audax* | *ut versus facerem.*)

[3] The authorities are Suetonius, who says *scriptum quaestoriun comparavit,* and the scholiasts to *Sat.* II. 6. 36.

[4] *Epist.* I. 19. 23—25 (*Parios ego primus iambos* | *ostendi Latio*). The oldest of the published works is *Sat.* I. 7, which seems to have been written in B.C. 43 or early in 42. *Epode* 16 seems to have been written on hearing the news of the capture of Perusia, B.C. 40. *Sat.* I. 2 and 4 were written before Horace became intimate with Maecenas. *Epode* 7 is assigned to B.C. 36.

[5] *Sat.* I. 6. 54, 55 (*optimus olim* | *Vergilius, post hunc Varius dixere quid essem*).

afterwards (B.C. 38)[1] Maecenas invited him to join his circle, and Horace's fortune was made.

C. Cilnius Maecenas was now and for long afterwards the right-hand man of Octavianus in all civil affairs. He was very rich, very fond of literary society, and very generous to literary men. His patronage relieved Horace from poverty and from anxiety about his social position, while it provided the necessary stimulus to a poet who was naturally both lazy and fastidious. The subsequent life of Horace has only a few prominent incidents. In the autumn of B.C. 38 he was one of a large party who accompanied Maecenas to Brundisium[2]. In B.C. 35 he published the first book of the Satires. Soon afterwards Maecenas gratified his dearest wish by presenting him with the small estate in the Sabine district[3], to which so many loving allusions are made in Horace's works. It seems to have been his habit, at least in later years, to spend the summer and autumn here[4], the winter at Baiae or Velia or some other seaside resort, and only the spring at Rome[5]. It is likely that Horace was present as a spectator at the battle of Actium in B.C. 31[6]. In B.C. 30 he published the second book of the Satires and, about the same time, the Epodes. About B.C. 23 he published the first three books of the Odes together.

It is obvious, in these works, that the political opinions of Horace had undergone a great change since he fought for the republic at Philippi. By B.C. 31 he had learnt to exult in the

---

[1] *Ibidem*, 61, 62 (*revocas nono post mense iubesque | esse in amicorum numero*). The year is fixed by *Sat.* II. 6. 40, 41, where Horace says that it is nearly eight years since *Maecenas me coepit habere suorum | in numero*. This satire was written at the end of B.C. 31.

[2] The journey is described in *Sat.* I. 5.

[3] The fullest description is in *Epist.* I. 16. The estate lay in the valley of the Digentia, north of Tibur.

[4] *Epist.* I. 16. 15, 16. (*hae latebrae dulces, etiam, si credis, amoenae, | incolumem tibi me praestant Septembribus horis.*)

[5] *Epist.* I. 7. 1—12.

[6] *Epod.* 1 and 9.

victory at Actium and to hail Caesar as the saviour of society[1]. But there is no sign, even as late as B.C. 20, when the first book of Epistles was published, that Horace was intimate with the emperor. Augustus was perhaps too busy, and too often absent from Rome[2], to cultivate the poet's acquaintance. But the intimacy, whenever it began[3], was of great importance to Horace. He yielded to Augustus what he had refused to Maecenas[4], and resumed the writing of lyric poetry, which he had meant to abandon. Thus in B.C. 17 he wrote the *Carmen Saeculare* by command, and about B.C. 14 the odes *Carm.* IV. 4 and 14, which formed the nucleus of the fourth book. Suetonius, who tells us this, tells us also that *Epist.* II. 1 was written at the express request of Augustus, who wished his name to be connected with a composition of this class[5].

The Fourth Book of the Odes was published about B.C. 14, the Second Book of the Epistles about B.C. 12[6]. It is observable that in these works the name of Maecenas is no longer prominent. The first Satire of the first book, the first Epode, the first Ode, the first Epistle had all been addressed to him in

---

[1] *Epod.* 9. *Carm.* I. 2 and 37.

[2] He was absent from Rome B.C. 31 to 29 and 27 to 24: was very ill in 23, and was absent again B.C. 22—19 (October).

[3] *Epist.* I. 9 shows that Horace had some acquaintance with Tiberius before B.C. 20, and perhaps *Epist.* I. 13 shows as much acquaintance with Augustus.

[4] *Epist.* I. 1.

[5] Suetonius says, "scripta quidem eius (Augustus) usque adeo probavit mansuraque perpetuo opinatus est, ut non modo saeculare carmen componendum iniunxerit, sed et Vindelicam victoriam Tiberii Drusique privignorum suorum, eumque coegerit propter hoc tribus carminum libris ex longo intervallo quartum addere: post sermones vero quosdam lectos nullam sui mentionem habitam ita sit questus 'irasci me tibi scito, quod non in plerisque eiusmodi scriptis mecum potissimum loquaris. An vereris ne apud posteros infame tibi sit, quod videaris familiaris nobis esse?' Expressitque eclogam ad se cuius initium est: '*Cum tot sustineas*,' etc."

[6] The date of the *Ars Poetica* is very uncertain.

grateful homage for his kindness, but there is no allusion to
him in the later publications save an affectionate record of his
birthday in *Carm.* IV. II. It is known, from Tacitus (*Ann.*
III. 30), that after B.C. 20 there was a coolness between
Maecenas and Augustus[1]. It is clear, too, from Suetonius,
that Augustus made efforts to detach Horace from Maecenas,
first by offering him a secretaryship, which was declined, and
afterwards by encouraging him to familiarity and giving him
handsome presents[2]. One may imagine, therefore, that Horace
was in an awkward and unhappy position. He was not easy
with Augustus but dared not offend him, and perhaps his
compliance with the emperor's commands roused some jealousy
in Maecenas. But the estrangement, if there was one, between
the poet and his patron did not endure. On his deathbed,
Maecenas wrote to Augustus 'Horati Flacci, ut mei, memor
esto.' He died early in B.C. 8, and Horace followed him to the
grave in the same year, on November 27th.

Horace describes himself, in B.C. 20, as 'short, prematurely
grey, fond of the sunshine, quick-tempered but easily appeased[3].'
Some account of his daily habits in Rome and in the country

[1] Augustus had an intrigue with Maecenas' wife, Terentia, but
Tacitus does not mention this.

[2] The following extracts from Suetonius' life of Horace will suffice:
'Augustus epistularum quoque officium obtulit, ut hoc ad Maecenatem
scripto significat: 'ante ipse sufficiebam scribendis epistulis amicorum,
nunc occupatissimus et infirmus Horatium nostrum a te cupio abducere.
Veniet ergo ab ista parasitica mensa ad hanc regiam, et nos in epistulis
scribendis adiuvabit.' Ac ne recusanti quidem aut succensuit quicquam
aut amicitiam suam ingerere desiit. Exstant epistulae e quibus argumenti
gratia pauca subieci: 'sume tibi aliquid iuris apud me, tanquam si
convictor mihi fueris; recte enim et non temere feceris quoniam id usus
mihi tecum esse volui, si per valetudinem tuam fieri possit.'...Praeterea
saepe...homuncionem lepidissimum adpellat unaque et altera liberalitate
locupletavit.' Horace had, in his later years, a house at Tibur, which
was still shown in Suetonius' time. This is supposed to have been
presented to him by Augustus.

[3] *Epist.* I. 20. 24, 25 (*corporis exigui, praecanum, solibus aptum,* |
irasci celerem, tamen ut placabilis essem).

is given in *Sat.* I. 6 and II. 6.   He suffered from dyspepsia and
gout or rheumatism, which caused fits of despondency (*Epist.*
I. 7 and 8).   Even without this information about his health, we
might easily infer from his poems that he was not a man of a
hearty and energetic temperament.

Of the other Augustan poets in whom we are most interested,
Horace certainly knew and loved and admired Vergil by far the
best (see esp. *C.* I. 3).   He was perhaps familiar with Tibullus (see
C. I. 33 and *Epist.* I. 4), though Tibullus belonged to the literary
circle of Messalla, not to that of Maecenas.   He must have known
and frequently met Propertius, who was another of Maecenas'
protégés, but for some reason there was no love lost between the
two men.   Neither mentions the other, but, if Propertius was not
the poet whose impertinence is described in *Sat.* I. 9, it is pretty
clear that he was the poet whose vanity is criticised in *Epist.* II.
2. 87 sqq. (See Postgate, *Select Elegies* of Prop. p. xxxii.)   Ovid,
who was a friend of Propertius, once actually rebukes Horace
(*A. A.* II. 271) and omits him from the list of entertaining poets
(*A. A.* III. 329—340), though he pays him a tardy compliment
after his death (*Trist.* IV. 10. 49).

§ 2.   *Chronology of the Odes.*

It is generally believed, though it is hardly certain, that the
first three books of the Odes were published together.   Suetonius (*supra* p. xiv *n.*) says only that Augustus required Horace
to add a fourth book long after the previous three had been
published.   But internal evidence is strongly in favour of the
received opinion.   Thus (1) the first ode of the series (I. 1) is
addressed to Maecenas, the last but one (III. 29) is also
addressed to Maecenas, and the last (III. 30) is a sort of *envoi*,
the poet congratulating himself upon his own achievement.
The first book of the Epistles is constructed on just this plan.
The first letter and the last but one are addressed to Maecenas,
the last is a humorous farewell, committing the book to the

world. (2) No ode in the first three Books points clearly to a later date than B.C. 24. On the other hand, there are odes in all three Books which refer to this and earlier dates. Thus III. 14 relates to the return of Augustus from Spain: I. 24 to the death of Quintilius: and I. 29 to the expedition of Aelius Gallus into Arabia. All these events happened in B.C. 24. II. 4 was written near the end of Horace's fortieth year, i.e. B.C. 25. I. 31, II. 15 and III. 6 seem all to refer to the restoration of temples which occupied Augustus in B.C. 28. It is obvious that these odes could have been published together. (3) The first Book cannot have been published before B.C. 24, for it refers, as we have just seen, to events of that year. If the second and third Books were written (in part) and published later, why does Horace, about B.C. 20 (see *Epist.* I. 1. 1—10), speak as if he had long given up the practice of writing lyrics and could not resume it?

If, then, we assume that the first three Books were published together, they must have been published late in B.C. 24 or early in B.C. 23. This date is inferred from the fact that Marcellus, the nephew and adopted son of Augustus, is referred to as the hope of the Caesarian house in *Carm.* I. 12. 45—48; and Licinius Murena, brother-in-law of Maecenas, is addressed in *Carm.* II. 10 and referred to as living in III. 19. Marcellus died in the autumn of B.C. 23, and Murena was executed for conspiracy in B.C. 22. It is not likely that Horace published these references to them after their deaths.

The only other dates proposed are B.C. 19 and B.C. 22. The former date is suggested because I. 3 is supposed to refer to the voyage which Vergil took, to Greece, early in B.C. 19; and other odes, especially II. 9, are thought to refer to the expedition into Armenia of B.C. 20. The date of II. 9, however, seems to be fixed to the end of B.C. 25, or the beginning of 24, by the allusion to *tropaea Augusti Caesaris*, a grand monument so called, voted by the Senate in B.C. 25. (See the concluding note on II. 9.) As to I. 3, it is likely that this ode does not refer to Vergil's last voyage to Greece, for it says nothing about Vergil's ill-health.

The date B.C. 22 was proposed by the late Prof. Sellar because, in Epist. I. 13, Horace, who was sending his odes to Augustus, directs the messenger (one Vinnius Asina) to push on over hills, rivers and bogs, as if Augustus were far away at the time. Prof. Sellar guessed that Augustus was in Sicily or Asia, whither he went in B.C. 22. It is just as likely, however, that Augustus was at Gabii, undergoing the cold-water treatment which cured him of a grave illness in B.C. 23.

(b) *The Fourth Book.* The fourth book of the Odes was beyond question written some years after the first three. The opening ode itself, the language of *Epist.* I. I. 1—10, and the express evidence of Suetonius (see p. xiv and *n.*) show that, after the publication of the first three Books, Horace had meant to abandon lyric composition, and only resumed it with reluctance. In the first ode, Horace describes himself as near 50 years of age. Odes 4 and 14 cannot have been written before the winter of B.C. 15, for they celebrate the grand campaign of that year in which Drusus conquered the Vindelici, Tiberius the Raeti. Ode 5 must have been written about the same time, for it complains of the long absence of Augustus, who had gone to Gaul in B.C. 16. Ode 2, perhaps, is a little later, for it was written when Augustus seemed likely to return to Rome soon. As a matter of fact, Augustus returned in July B.C. 13. It seems probable therefore that the book was published in B.C. 14 or early in 13. (On the metrical peculiarities of Book IV. see *infra* pp. xxviii, xxix and the first note to *C.* IV.)

§ 3. *Some Characteristics of Horace's Poetry.*

The Odes of Horace are avowedly imitations of Greek models: but there were Greek models of two quite different kinds, and Horace sometimes imitated them both at the same time. On the one hand, there were *public* odes, such as Pindar (B.C. 480) wrote—dithyrambs, paeans, songs of victory and dirges—solemn and elaborate compositions, intended to be sung by a trained chorus who danced or marched while they sang. On the other hand, there were lyrics such as Alcaeus or

Sappho or Anacreon wrote—songs intended to be sung by one person in a private circle[1].

The lyrics of Horace (though they were meant to be read or recited, not sung) belong entirely in form, and usually in substance, to the latter class. His metres are all borrowed from the Greek song-writers, and his Muse, as he often says, was inclined to be sportive (*iocosa*) rather than solemn[2]. Even in the *Carmen Saeculare* and in *Carm.* IV. 6, which were written for public performance by a chorus, he did not attempt the grand Pindaric elaboration which, he confesses indeed (*Carm.* IV. 2. 25—32), was beyond him. Yet several of the longer and graver odes (see especially III. 3, 4, 5, 11, 27, IV. 4), though still written in song-metres, are quite Pindaric in the treatment of the theme. In III. 3, for instance, the opening truism, the illustrations from many myths, the elaborate invention of Juno's compact and the brief sententious close are all clear imitations of Pindar[3]. The Pindaric tendency, here

---

[1] *Ars Poet.* 83—85. *Musa dedit fidibus divos puerosque deorum | et pugilem victorem et equum certamine primum | et iuvenum curas et libera vina referre.* Of these lines the first two refer to choral odes, and the third to songs. Lyrical poetry intended for a chorus is sometimes called *melic.*

[2] See *Carm.* I. 6: II. 1. 37 and 12. 1—5, 12—16: III. 3. 69: IV. 2 and 15.

[3] The extant odes of Pindar are all 'epinikia,' i.e. celebrations of the victories of certain persons in the great athletic contests of Greece. The following summary of the First Olympian Ode will sufficiently show Pindar's manner of treating a theme:

1—15. Water is the best drink: gold the choicest metal: so are the Olympic games the noblest games.

15—38. Let us sing the praises of Hiero, the victor, who won glory at Olympia, the home of Pelops.

38—55. Song can give currency to falsehoods, but we must not speak evil of deities.

56—85. Poseidon, of his great love, carried off Pelops. The tale that Pelops was killed and eaten is a base invention.

86—150. Because of the misdeeds of his father Tantalus, Pelops

conspicuously seen, to wander into mythology may be noticed too in many of the shorter pieces (e.g. *Carm.* I. 7, 18: II. 4, 13: III. 17: IV. 6). It should be remembered, however, that, in an ode of Pindar, composed for a religious and patriotic festival, a fine local myth, showing forth 'the glories of our birth and state,' was especially appropriate; and that moralizing too was, in Pindar's day, as much expected of the poet as fine images and musical rhythms. He was the popular philosopher, the seer who could discern the tendencies of men's actions and could pronounce upon them with due blame or praise.

Horace derived, then, from his Greek models a certain discursiveness in his treatment of a theme. He took from them also an extreme 'abruptness' of manner, such that it is often difficult to follow the train of his thoughts (see, for instance, I. 7 or II. 2 or III. 4 or IV. 9). This abruptness is due partly to the brevity of his diction and partly to a literary convention. As the poet Gray wrote to his friend Mason, 'extreme conciseness of expression, yet pure, perspicuous and musical, is one of the great beauties of lyric poetry.' And the reason is obvious. In short lines, with a marked rhythmical beat, almost every word becomes emphatic and must deserve to be emphatic. This conciseness necessarily leads to abruptness of thought, for the conjunctions and brief explanatory phrases which, in a freer style of composition, serve to mark the connexion of ideas, are excluded from lyrics by their unemphatic character. It is a convention also, between poets and their audience, that lyrics, however elaborate, should profess to be written on the inspiration of the moment, and should therefore seem to be hurried, unpremeditated, unmethodical. They are spoilt if they become argumentative.

In real inspiration Horace was probably deficient. Certainly

was sent back to earth and, by help of Poseidon, he won Hippodamia to wife in a chariot-race at Olympia.

150—160. From that time forth the glory of the Olympian races has shone abroad.

161—184. I sing the victor, Hiero, wisest and greatest of kings. Win again, Hiero, and be thou first among kings, I among poets.

his poems are not, to use Wordsworth's phrase, 'the sponta-
neous overflow of powerful feeling.' He himself describes them
as laborious (*operosa carmina C.* IV. 2. 31). But they are sincere,
that is to say, they are the genuine expression of his thoughts and
sentiments ; and if they do not reveal to us a man of profound
insight or ardent passions or lofty imagination, they show at
least sympathy, affection, humour, a generous admiration of
great men and noble deeds, and a sturdy pride in his vocation.
And a man with these qualities, if his vocation happens to be
literature, has always been sure of a lasting success. The tact
which results from his sympathy and humour appears in his
style as well as in his matter, and his writings have the charm
which is recognized as 'companionable.' In our own country,
Addison and Lamb, in France, Montaigne and Mme. de
Sévigné, are conspicuous examples of the Horatian temperament and of its enduring popularity. And Horace had the
advantage of writing in verse and of using a language which
gave the utmost assistance to his special literary talent. 'The
best words in the best places' is a definition of poetry that
Coleridge was fond of repeating. It might serve for a description of Horace's writing. He was gifted by nature with a fine
ear and an infinite capacity for taking pains, and he had had
a scholarly education. He borrowed, from Greek, metres of
peculiar swing, and he had, in his native Latin, a store of
sonorous and pregnant words, a terse and lucid grammar, and
the liberty to arrange his words to the best advantage. With
these resources, he has produced an incomparable series of
brilliant phrases ('jewels five words long' Tennyson calls them)
which are at once easy to remember and impossible to translate[1].

[1] It is idle to quote instances where almost every line is an instance,
but one might choose *simplex munditiis* or *insaniens sapientia* or
splendide mendax as examples of Horace's untranslateable brevity:
dulce et decorum est pro patria mori or *nihil est ab omni parte beatum* as
examples of finished commonplace: *non indecoro pulvere sordidos* or
intaminatis fulget honoribus or *impavidum ferient ruinae* as specimens
of sonority, and *qui fragilem truci commisit pelago ratem* as an instance
of the artful arrangement of contrasted words.

To a writer with this faculty, it matters little that his ideas are scanty and commonplace. His readers have the less trouble in understanding him and agreeing with him, and can surrender themselves to the charm of his diction. It is because we all find in Horace 'what oft was thought but ne'er so well express'd' that he has been used, for so many ages, as the indispensable model of literary excellence.

§ 4. *Some Characteristics of Horace's Latinity.*

Horace's Latin is a good deal affected by the conciseness which, as we have just said (p. xx) was demanded by the perpetually recurring emphases of lyric poetry. For the sake of brevity he often used expressions which may be called 'short cuts,' intended to avoid unemphatic prepositions and conjunctions, and to bring important words closer together. The most striking instances of this practice are his use of the genitive case and of the infinitive mood. His freedom in the use of these constructions was undoubtedly imitated from the Greek, though it is not always possible to produce a Greek parallel for every Horatian instance.

1. The following are examples, in the Odes, of unusual genitives: *diva potens Cypri* (I. 3. I), *agrestium regnavit populorum* (III. 30. 11), *desine querelarum* (II. 9. 17, 18), *abstineto irarum* (III. 27. 69, 70), *integer vitae scelerisque purus* (I. 22. I), *patriae exul* (II. 16. 19), *prosperam frugum* (IV. 6. 39), *fertilis frugum* (*Carm. Saec.* 29), *fecunda culpae* (III. 6. 17), *pauper aquae* (III. 30. II), *dives artium* (IV. 8. 5), *docilis modorum* (IV. 6. 43), probably also *notus animi paterni* (II. 2. 6, though these words need not be construed together)[1].

2. The infinitive mood is often used by Horace, as it is often used in Greek, where in prose a final or a consecutive

---

[1] The Greek constructions imitated are such as βασιλεύειν Πύλου, λήγειν ἀοιδῆς, ἀγνὸς αἵματος, φυγὰς Ἄργους, πλούσιος χρυσίου, μαθητικὸς μουσικῆς, θαυμάζειν τινὰ τοῦ νοῦ.

clause (with *ut* and the subj.) would be required[1]. Some of the instances in Horace (e.g. *certat tollere* in I. I. 6, or *gaudet posuisse* I. 34. 16, or *tendentes imposuisse* III. 4. 52) can be paralleled in prose, but the following are extremely bold : *pecus egit visere* (I. 2. 8), *coniurata rumpere* and *furit reperire* (I. 15. 7 and 27), *te persequor frangere* (I. 23. 10), *tradam ventis portare* (I. 26. 3), *laborat trepidare* (II. 3. 11), *urges summovere* (II. 18. 21), *dedit spernere* (II. 16. 39), *impulerit maturare necem* (III. 7. 14—16), *me expetit urere* (*Epod.* 11. 5).

The infinitive is similarly used with adjectives to suggest a purpose or consequence, or to limit the aspect of the epithet[2] : as *indocilis pati* (I. 1. 18), *callidus condere* (I. 10. 7), *blandus ducere* I. 12. 11, 12), *praesens tollere* and *dolosus ferre* (I. 35. 2 and 28), *leviora tolli* (II. 4. 11), *pertinax ludere* (III. 29. 53), *efficax eluere* (IV. 12. 20), *veraces cecinisse* (Carm. Saec. 25), *lubricus aspici* (I. 19. 8), *niveus videri* (IV. 2. 59), *nefas videre* (Epod. 16. 14), *nobilis superare* (I. 12. 26), and *dolens vinci* (IV. 4. 62.)

It is obvious that, in many of these instances, a gerund with or without a preposition might have been used. Horace, however, regards the infinitive (in the Greek way) as an indeclinable noun.

These constructions, though found in other Latin poets, are specially characteristic of Horace ; but, besides these, he has many other and more common devices to procure that perpetual quaintness which, as Aristotle said, is essential to poetical diction.

3. With adjectives, he is partial to a kind of *hypallage*

---

[1] The Greek constructions imitated are such as ἀνὴρ χαλεπὸς συζῆν, παρέχω ἐμαυτὸν τῷ ἰατρῷ τέμνειν, θαῦμα ἰδέσθαι, λευκὸς ὁρᾶσθαι.

[2] In the instances above cited, grammarians would call some of the infinitives *prolate* or *complementary*, others *epexegetical* or *explanatory*. The difference between the two kinds is briefly this: the prolate infin. is necessary to limit the meaning of the preceding verb or adjective, while the epexegetical infin. is merely illustrative of the meaning. E.g. *celer irasci* means 'quick to anger,' not 'quick at everything, anger included,' whereas *blandus ducere quercus* does mean 'persuasive to everything, oaks included.'

(i.e. 'inversion of relations'), whereby an epithet is transferred from the producer to the thing produced or vice versa.

Of the first case, *iracunda fulmina* (I. 3. 40), *dementes ruinas* (I. 37. 7), *iratos apices* (III. 21. 19), *invido flatu* (IV. 5. 9), are good enough examples. Instances of the second case are more interesting, because here the meaning of the adjective is somewhat affected. Thus *nigri venti* (I. 5. 7) means, in effect, 'blackening winds,' and *albus* (I. 7. 15) or *candidus* (III. 7. 1), applied to a wind, means 'clearing,' 'brightening.' Similar examples are *palma nobilis* (I. 1. 5), *decorae palaestrae* (I. 10. 4), *insigni Camena* (I. 12. 39), *inaequales procellae* (II. 9. 3), *informes hiemes* (II. 10. 5).

Horace is somewhat free in his use of adjectives in *-bilis* or *-ilis*. Thus *flebilis* (I. 24. 9), *amabilis* (II. 9. 13), *docilis* (III. 11. 1 and IV. 6. 43), are equivalent to *defletus, amatus, doctus*. On the other hand, passive participles, such as *irruptus* (I. 13. 18), *indomitus* (II. 14. 2), *intaminatus* (III. 2. 18), often supply the place of an adjective in *-bilis*.

4. The neuter sing. of an adjective is sometimes used as an adverb: as *dulce ridentem* (I. 22. 23), *lucidum fulgentes* (II. 12. 14), *perfidum ridens* (III. 27. 67), *turbidum laetatur* (II. 19. 6).

5. A few words not used elsewhere (ἅπαξ λεγόμενα) occur in the Odes. Such are *inaudax* (III. 20. 3), *exultim* (III. 11. 10), *immetatus* (III. 24. 12), *Faustitas* (IV. 5. 18), *inemori* (Epod. 5. 34).

6. The dative case is many times used for *in* with accus. after a verb of sending: e.g. *terris misit* (I. 2. 1), *mittes lucis* (I. 12. 60), *compulerit gregi* (I. 24. 18), *caelo tuleris* (III. 23. 1), and a similar use may be suspected elsewhere (*e.g. C.* II. 7. 16, IV. 1. 7).

7. Of strange ablatives *Cecropio cothurno* in II. 1. 12 and *coniuge barbara* in III. 5. 5 are conspicuous instances. Abl. of the agent without *ab* occurs perhaps in I. 6. 1 (where see note).

8. Certain oddities in the arrangement of words may also be noticed.

(*a*) An epithet, really qualifying two words, is often put with the second only. E.g. in I. 2. 1 *nivis atque dirae grandinis*: 5. 5 *fidem mutatosque deos*: also I. 31. 16 : 34. 8 : II. 8. 3 : 19. 24 : III. 2. 16 : 11. 39 : IV. 14. 4.

(*b*) Similarly, a verb, which belongs to both parts of a compound sentence, is often inserted in the second part with -*que* or -*ve*: e.g. I. 30. 6 *Gratiae properentque nymphae*: II. 7. 24 *apio curatve myrto*. Also II. 17. 16 : 19. 28, 31 : III. 4. 12 : *Carm. Saec.* 22.

(*c*) Sentences in which a word may be constructed with either of two other words—the so-called construction ἀπὸ κοινοῦ or 'in common'—are frequent. A striking instance is in II. 18. 37 *hic levare functum* | *pauperem laboribus* | *vocatus atque non vocatus audit*. Here *laboribus* is appropriate to *levare* and to *functum*: and *levare* is appropriate to *vocatus* and to *audit*. So in II. 11. 11 *consiliis* may be constructed with *minorem* and *fatigas*: and in III. 8. 19 *sibi* with *infestus* or *dissidet*.

That the Romans found something inimitable in Horace's style is evident from the rarity and badness of the attempts to imitate him. The few pieces of sapphics and alcaics in Statius and Ausonius are almost doggrel.

§ 5. *Metres of the Odes.*

The first eleven odes of the 1st Book comprise examples of nearly all the metres used by Horace in the Odes. The only novelties introduced in later books are the Hipponactic stanza of II. 18, the Archilochian of IV. 7 and the Ionic of III. 12.

Metre, in Latin and Greek, is the arrangement of long and short syllables in a line of poetry.

Rhythm is the arrangement of stresses (*ictus*) or loud syllables. In other words, metre is the mode of constructing a line : rhythm is the mode of reading or singing it[1].

For purposes of metre, all long syllables are alike, and all short syllables are alike : but for purposes of rhythm (as in music) long syllables may be of different lengths, and short syllables may be of different lengths.

---

[1] In English metre and rhythm are identical, for with us a syllable which has stress is long, and a syllable which has no stress is short.

In Horace's Odes, we know the metres, but we do not know the rhythms. In other words we do not know how Horace himself would have read and scanned his lines. For instance, the First Ode of the First Book consists of lines of this metre: $- - - \cup \cup - - \cup \cup - \cup \bar{\cup}$. But the lines may be scanned and read in several different ways: thus

   (1) Maéce | nás ata | vís | édite | régi | bús.
   (2) Maéce | nás atavis | édite reg | ibús.
   (3) Maéce | nás ata | vís | édite | régibus.
   (4) Maécenas at | avís edi | te régibus.

Of these methods, the first represents the original Greek rhythm: the second, the scansion which was adopted by grammarians nearly contemporary with Horace: the third, a possible scansion which occurs naturally to an English reader: the fourth is an old-fashioned method which is seldom mentioned now, but which has some merits.

That Horace usually employed the second method, is rendered probable by such lines as

     exegi monumentum aere perennius   (III. 30. 1)
or   *perrupit Acheronta Herculeus labor*   (I. 3. 36):

still more by such a line as

     dum flagrantia detorquet ad oscula (II. 12. 25).

These instances suggest that there was not such a pause on the sixth syllable as is required by the first method or the third.

But it would seem that, in this matter of 'pause,' Horace was not likely to be consistent. Witness his treatment of *synapheia.*

Synapheia is the 'connexion' of line with line, so that (among other effects) a syllable liable to elision may not conclude a line if the next line begins with a vowel. Horace, as a rule, follows the Greek lyrists in maintaining synapheia, and several times elides a concluding syllable before a vowel at the beginning of the next line, or divides a word between two lines. See, for elision, II. 2. 11 : 3. 27 : 16. 34 : III. 29. 35 : IV. 1. 35 : 2. 22 and 23 : *Carm. Saec.* 47 : and, for division, I. 2. 19 : 25. 11 : II. 16. 7. But in I. 2. 41 and 47 : I. 8. 3 : I. 12. 6 and 7, and many other places, synapheia is ignored and hiatus permitted. Hiatus, of course, implies a slight pause, while synapheia implies that there was no pause between two lines.

For reasons such as these, it is impossible to put forward an authoritative scansion to Horace's lines. In the metrical schemes here subjoined no scansion will be suggested, but the original (i.e. the Greek) rhythm will be given in musical notation according to the theories of Dr J. H. H. Schmidt[1]. It will be seen that Dr Schmidt divides a line into bars of equal length, i.e. occupying the same time in delivery.

In the metrical schemes, a comma marks the caesura or diaeresis, i.e. the point which must coincide with the end of a word[2].

It remains to be added that all the odes of Horace seem to be divisible into stanzas of four lines. The only exceptions are IV. 8, which there are many reasons for rejecting in whole or in part: and III. 12, which consists of four periods of ten feet each. The metres were undoubtedly borrowed by Horace from the Greek lyrists, especially Alcaeus, but he has introduced many small alterations, such as the use of long syllables where the Greeks allowed shorts, and the regular use of caesura where the Greeks had none.

    I.   The **Alcaic** stanza is used in 37 odes, viz.:

        I.   9. 16. 17. 26. 27. 29. 31. 34. 35. 37.

      II.   1. 3. 5. 7. 9. 11. 13. 14. 15. 17. 19. 20.

    III.   1. 2. 3. 4. 5. 6. 17. 21. 23. 26. 29.

    IV.   4. 9. 14. 15.

---

[1] *Rhythmic and Metric of the Classical Languages*, translated by Dr J. W. White.

[2] Technically, *caesura* is the division of a foot between two words, so that part of the foot belongs to one word, the remainder to another. *Diaeresis*, on the other hand, is the division of feet from one another so that one foot ends with a word, while the next begins a new word. Thus, in the bucolic hexameter, there is caesura in the third foot and diaeresis between the fourth and fifth : as

        Nos patri | ae fi | nes et | dulcia | linquimus | arva.

The metrical scheme is:

1, 2. ⌣ – ◡ – –, – ◡ ◡ – ◡ ⊐ (eleven syllables).

3. ⌣ – ◡ – – – ◡ – ⊐ (nine syllables).

4. – ◡◡ – ◡◡ – ◡ – ⊐ (ten syllables).

The first two lines begin with a short syllable only 18 times (out of 634 examples)[1].

The diaeresis (which was not used by the Greeks) after the fifth syllable is neglected in I. 16. 21: 37. 5: 37. 14: II. 17. 21: IV. 14. 17. Elision occurs at the diaeresis in III. 1. 5: 4. 49. The fifth syllable is short in III. 5. 17: and possibly III. 23. 18.

In the third line, the first syllable is short only 10 times in 317 examples. The fifth syllable is, in Horace, always long, though in Alcaeus it appears to have been always short. A most important rule in the construction of this line is that it shall not end with two dissyllabic words. Such an ending occurs only 8 times, viz. I. 16. 4: 26. 7: 29. 11: II. 1. 11: 13. 27: 14. 11: 19. 7: 19. 11: and in 5 of these eight instances, the first dissyllable is repeated at the beginning of the next line (e.g. II. 13. 27 *dura navis | dura fugae mala*).

In the fourth line, there is usually caesura after the fourth syllable, but the main rule is that the line shall not begin with two trisyllabic words (e.g. *tristia tempora*).

Synapheia of the third and fourth lines occurs in II. 3. 27: III. 29. 35, but is conspicuously neglected in I. 16. 27: 17. 13: II. 13. 7. Yet, on the whole, synapheia is usually respected. 'An Alcaic line does not often end with a short vowel, even when the next line begins with a consonant.' (Ramsay, *Latin Prosody*, p. 212.)

The original rhythm, according to Dr Schmidt, was:

---

[1] In the IVth Book, the opening syllable is always long.

This rhythm is trochaic, with an *anacrusis* (or 'striking-up' syllable) at the beginning of lines 1, 2, 3.

2. The **Sapphic** stanza is used in 25 odes, viz.:

I.   2. 10. 12. 20. 22. 25. 30. 32. 38.
II. 2. 4. 6. 8. 10. 16.
III. 8. 11. 14. 18. 20. 22. 27.
IV. 2. 6. 11 and *Carmen Saeculare.*

The stanza seems to have been invented by Alcaeus, though it is named after Sappho. The metrical scheme is:

1, 2, 3. $- \cup - - -, \cup \cup - \cup - \overline{\cup}$ (eleven syllables).
4. $- \cup \cup - \overline{\cup}$ (five syllables).

The longer line is called *the lesser Sapphic:* the shorter the *Adonius.*

In the longer line Horace always has the fourth syllable long, whereas Sappho (and Catullus) often had it short.

Horace has also introduced a caesura, which was not used by Sappho. This caesura, in the first three Books, generally occurs after the 5th syllable, and only occasionally after the 6th (e.g. I. 10. 1, 6, 18), but in the fourth Book and *Carm. Saec.* it is very frequently placed after the 6th syllable (in fact, 39 times in only four compositions).

Synapheia is obviously respected between the 2nd and 3rd lines in II. 2. 18: 16. 34: IV. 2. 22; where final syllables are elided: and between the 3rd and 4th lines in I. 2. 19: 25. 11: II. 16. 7: IV. 2. 23: *Carm. Saec.* 47, where either a word is divided (as in the first three passages) or a syllable elided (as in the last two).

Yet hiatus between the lines frequently occurs, as in I. 2. 41 and 47: 12. 6 and 7 etc.

The original rhythm, according to Dr Schmidt, was trochaic and may be represented thus:

3. A stanza called the *Greater Sapphic* is used in I. 8. It consists of couplets of the following form:

1, 3. $-\cup\cup-\cup-\overline{\cup}$.

2, 4. $-\cup---, \cup\cup-, -\cup\cup-\cup-\underset{\smile}{\times}$.

It will be seen that the first line is longer by two syllables than the Adonius, and the second line is longer by four ($-\cup\cup-$) than the lesser Sapphic.

The original rhythm is said to be:

4. The metres called **Asclepiad** are founded on the following lines:

    (*a*) $---\cup\cup-, -\cup\cup-\cup\underset{\smile}{\times}$ ('lesser Asclepiad').

    (*b*) $---\cup\cup-, -\cup\cup-, -\cup\cup-\cup\underset{\smile}{\times}$ ('greater Asclepiad').

    (*c*) $---\cup\cup-\cup\underset{\smile}{\times}$ ('Glyconic').

    (*d*) $---\cup\cup--$ ('Pherecratic').

In the Lesser Asclepiad, the caesura is neglected in II. 12. 25 and IV. 8. 17. A short syllable is lengthened at the caesura in I. 13. 6: III. 16. 26.

In the Greater Asclepiad there are two caesuras, but the second is neglected in I. 18. 16.

In the Glyconic, the second syllable is perhaps short in I. 15. 24 and 36.

These lines are combined by Horace into four-line stanzas of different kinds thus:

(A) The *First Asclepiad* stanza employs (*a*) alone. See I. 1, III. 30, IV. 8.

(B) The *Second Asclepiad* has (*b*) alone. See I. 11 and 18: IV. 10.

(C) The *Third Asclepiad* has couplets of (*a*) and (*c*). See I. 3. 13. 19. 36. III. 9. 15. 19. 24. 25. 28. IV. 1. 3.

(D) The *Fourth Asclepiad* has (*a*) thrice repeated, followed by (*c*). See I. 6. 15. 24. 33. II. 12. III. 10. 16. IV. 5. 12.

(E) The *Fifth Asclepiad* has (*a*) twice repeated, then (*d*), then (*c*). See I. 5. 14. 21. 23. III. 7. 13. IV. 13.

The original rhythms are said to be:

(a) ♩ ♪ | ♪. ♪ ♪ | ♩. | ♪. ♪ ♪ | ♩ ♪ | ♩ ╕

(b) ♩ ♪ | ♪. ♪ ♪ | ♩. | ♪. ♪ ♪ | ♩. | ♪. ♪ ♪ | ♩ ♪ | ♩ ╕

(c) ♩ ♪ | ♪. ♪ ♪ | ♩ ♪ | ♩ ╕

(d) ♩ ♪ | ♪. ♪ ♪ | ♩ ♪.

5. The *Alcmanian* stanza is used in I. 7 and 28, and in Epode 12. It consists of couplets made up of an ordinary dactylic hexameter, followed by a dactylic tetrameter.

1, 3. $- \overline{\smile\smile} \mid - \overline{\smile\smile} \mid -, \overline{\smile\smile} \mid - \overline{\smile\smile} \mid - \smile\smile \mid - \underset{\smile}{-}.$

2, 4. $- \overline{\smile\smile} \mid - \overline{\smile\smile} \mid - \overline{\smile\smile} \mid - \underset{\smile}{-}.$

In the second line, there is usually a caesura in the second or third dactyl.

The rhythm is really dactylic, i.e. each dactyl is of the value ♩ ♪ ♪ and each spondee of the value ♩ ♩.

6. The other metres used in the Odes are exhibited only in single specimens, which are treated in the notes as they severally occur (see II. 18. III. 12. IV. 7). But the metre of I. 4 may be specially noticed here.

It is called the *Fourth Archilochian*, and consists of a four-line stanza in which the lines are arranged as follows :

1, 3. $- \overline{\smile\smile} - \overline{\smile\smile} -, \overline{\smile\smile} - \smile\smile, - \smile - \smile - -.$

2, 4. $\smile - \smile - \overline{\smile}, - \smile - \smile - -.$

The first line is called 'the greater Archilochian': the second is an 'iambic trimeter catalectic'[1].

This combination is so curious that Dr Schmidt thinks that Horace must have read the dactyls as ♪ ♪ ♪, not as ♩ ♪ ♪, so that the rhythm becomes trochaic, thus :

1, 3.

♪. ♪ ♪ | ♪. ♪ ♪ | ♪. ♪ ♪ | ♪. ♪ ♪ | ♩ ♪ | ♩ ♪ | ♩. ♩ ╕

2, 4.

♪ | ♩ ♪ | ♩ ♪ | ♩ ♪ | ♩ ♪ | ♩. | ♩ ╕

[1] A 'catalectic,' or 'stopping' line, is one which comes to an end in the middle of a foot.

§ 6. *Order of the Odes.*

Though there is some reason to suspect slight interpolations
in the Odes (see below, p. xxxiv), there is no reason for doubting
that the present arrangement of the poems is substantially that
of Horace himself. But the order is clearly not chronological:
e.g. I. 24 was written in B.C. 24, while III. 1—6 were written in
B.C. 27. Nor are poems of one kind, either in subject or metre,
placed together, for (e.g.) political poems and Alcaic odes occur
in all parts of the collection.

But we can often discern special reasons for placing single
odes or groups of odes in particular places. Thus I. 1, II. 20,
III. 29 and 30, IV. 1, are obviously appropriate to their places:
the six great odes at the beginning of Book III. form a definite
cycle, and it is not an accident that the first nine odes of Book
I. are specimens of nearly all the metres that Horace attempted,
or that the first three odes are addressed to Maecenas, Augustus
and Vergil.

In regard to the bulk of the poems, however, it is likely that
Horace deliberately threw them into some confusion in order to
favour that appearance of inspiration and unpremeditatedness
which, as was noticed above (p. xx), was one of the conventions
of lyrical composition. His Muse, he would have us believe,
was a whimsical lady, but we may say of her, as Congreve said
of Fair Amoret,

> "Careless she is with artful care,
> Affecting to seem unaffected."

One noticeable device for securing this effect was to place in
juxtaposition odes written in different moods, the grave with the
gay, the lively with the severe (e.g. I. 12 and 13, 24 and 25, 37 and
38: II. 3 and 4: III. 6 and 7). Another is to pretend that the
casual thought of one ode suggested the whole theme of the
next, as the mention of Fortune in I. 34 suggests I. 35, and the
mention of a holiday in III. 17 suggests III. 18. Contrasts of
subject too are not infrequent, as where in II. 6 and 7 the quiet

stay-at-home life of Horace gives extra point to his welcome of
the wanderer Pompeius: and in III. 23 and 24 the praise of
simple piety leads up to a denunciation of wealth.

§ 7. *The Text.*

Horace's works, as he himself prophesied (*Epist.* I. 20. 17,
18), soon became one of the regular Roman schoolbooks. They
were so in the time of Quintilian and Juvenal (say A.D. 100), and
remained so in the time of Ausonius (say A.D. 380). Vergil, too,
shared the same fate (see Mayor's note on Juvenal VII. 227).
But while of Vergil we have several MSS. complete or fragmentary, which date from a very high antiquity (earlier than A.D.
500), we have only one of Horace which is as old as the 9th
century. Most of the extant MSS. of Horace were written in
the 10th century or later.

Moreover, no extant MS. of Horace seems to have been
written in Italy. The oldest, called B (*Bernensis*, of the 9th
century), is a fragmentary copy written in Ireland. The others
appear to have been all written in France or Germany after that
revival of schools and of literary studies which Charlemagne
introduced with the assistance of Alcuin of York (about A.D.
820). There is evidence that Horace was well known to some
students at this time, though many years must have elapsed
before the reading of profane poets was permitted in the
cathedral schools of the German Empire. At Paderborn, for
instance, it was not till after A.D. 1000 that it could be said
'viguit *Horatius*, magnus et *Virgilius*, *Crispus* ac *Salustius* et
Urbanus Statius.' (See Maitland's *Dark Ages*, Nos. XI. and
VIII. and *Class. Review* 1894, p. 305.)

Of the extant MSS., other than B, the chief are Aφψλπ, all
now at Paris: δ and *d*, both in the British Museum: R, now in
the Vatican (though it was written in Alsace): *l* at Leyden: *a*
at Milan: *ν* at Dessau. All these, with some others, are
assigned to the 10th century, and there are many more of later
date.

Most of the oldest MSS. have been inspected by more than one editor, but the fullest collation will be found in the editions of O. Keller and A. Holder (see esp. their *editio minor* of 1879).

The text of Horace presented in these MSS. is not in a satisfactory state: that is to say, it leaves grave doubt, in very many places, as to what Horace really wrote. Apart from the numerous passages where we have two alternative readings, both good (see next page), there are places where there are alternatives both bad (e.g. III. 4. 10 *limen Apuliae*, or III. 24. 4 *mare Apulicum*, or Epod. 9. 17 *ad hunc*), and places where the MSS. are agreed but the reading can hardly be sound (e.g. I. 20. 10 *bibes*, I. 23. 5 *veris adventus*, II. 2. 2 *inimice*, III. 26. 7 *arcus*, IV. 2. 49 *teque*). And there are many places, too, where interpolation may reasonably be suspected: such as I. 31. 13—16, III. 11. 17—20, and IV. 8 (either the whole or part). In this matter it should be remembered that epigrams were interpolated in Martial's works in his own life-time (as he himself complains, e.g. I. 54, X. 100), and that Horace, being a schoolbook, was especially liable to interpolation. A good schoolmaster, for instance, in commenting on Horace's style, would doubtless compose a stanza now and again, to show the trick of it, and some of these imitations, written in the margin of the text, with other notes for lessons, might easily pass into the text itself[1].

The question, however, whether a certain stanza is interpolated, or a certain reading is good enough for Horace, must always remain open, unless some more authoritative MS. is discovered. But the existing MSS. undoubtedly prove that the text of Horace was, in very ancient times, doubtful, and was emended by good scholars. A considerable number of our

---

[1] It is observable, here, that in the Appendix on prosody to the *Ars Grammatica* of Diomedes, a grammarian of the 4th century, only 35 Odes are ascribed to Bk. I. (omitting 22, 25, 35): only 19 to Bk. II. (omitting 16), and only 25 to Bk. III. The Harleian MS. No. 2724, in the British Museum, has at the end some Sapphics beginning

> Flante cum terram Zephyro solutam
> Floribus vestit redimita terra.

MSS. contain, at the end of the Epodes, the following *sub-scriptio*:

Vettius Agorius Basilius Mavortius v.c. et inl. (vir consularis et inlustris) *ex cõm. dõm.* (ex comite domestico) *ex cõns. õrd.* (ex consule ordinario) *legi et ut potui emendavi conferente mihi Magistro Felice oratore urbis Romae.*

This Mavortius was consul A.D. 527, and probably edited both the odes and the epodes. Unfortunately, it is not possible to restore his edition even from the MSS. which bear his *sub-scriptio*, for these MSS. differ from one another at most of the crucial points. But it is plain that our copies are descended from two editions of Horace, that of Mavortius for one, and another of which we do not know the origin. These editions differed from one another in a great number of single words: e.g.

Carminum, I.	4.	8	*visit, urit.*
	18.	5	*increpat, crepat.*
	27.	13	*voluptas, voluntas.*
	28.	15	*mors, nox.*
	32.	1	*poscimus, poscimur.*
	35.	17	*saeva, serva.*
II.	3.	28	*exitium, exilium.*
	13.	8	*laborem, laborum.*
	20.	13	*ocior, notior.*
III.	3.	34	*ducere, discere.*
	5.	37	*aptius, inscius.*
	8.	27	*rape, cape.*
	14.	6	*divis, sacris.*
	15.	2	*fige, pone.*
	19.	27	*Rhode, Chloe.*
	23.	19	*mollivit, mollibit.*
	27.	48	*monstri, tauri.*
	29.	34	*aequore, alveo.*
IV.	2.	58	*ortum, orbem.*
	4.	36	*dedecorant, indecorant.*
	7.	17	*vitae, summae.*
	13.	14	*cari, clari.*
	14.	28	*meditatur, minitatur.*

Epodon,   2. 25 *ripis, rivis.*
           5. 15 *implicata, illigata.*
           5. 58 *suburanae, suburbanae.*
          16. 61 *astri, austri.*
          17. 11 *unxere, luxere.*
          17. 64 *láboribus, doloribus.*
Carmen Saeculare,   23 *totiens, totidem.*
           65 *arces, aras.*

In these instances (and many more might have been given) there is usually little to be said in favour of one reading and against the other, and the MSS. are very fairly divided between the two. But the MSS. which agree in one reading do not agree in the next, and very often indeed both readings together are recorded in the same MS.

One or two examples will illustrate the extreme perplexity of the authorities. In *C.* I. 2. 18 the absurd reading *jactat velorum* (for *ultorem*) appears in seven MSS. φψλδzπ. It would naturally be supposed that these MSS. were derived from one source, but in I. 4. 8, λlπ read *urit* while φψδz read *visit* (which λl also record as a variant). In I. 9. 6 φψδπ have the absurd reading *largiri potis* for *large reponens*, but in 8. 2 δπ have *hoc deos oro*, while φψ have *te deos oro*. Again, only three MSS. λlu omit the line I. 5. 13, but 12. 26, which is also omitted in λl, is not omitted in *u*, but is omitted in δzπL. One is perpetually baffled by difficulties of this kind in attempting to trace the history and connexions of our MSS. It would seem that the monks, who wrote our copies, had more than one text before them, or one text smothered with notes and corrections, and as most of the copies were made about the same time, it is impossible to distinguish two or three of them as being the source, or as representing the source, of all the rest.

A very large body of marginal notes or *scholia* on Horace has come down to us. They are in the main derived from two commentaries on Horace, written by Pomponius Porphyrion and Helenius Acron. Porphyrion appears to have lived about A.D. 200, and Acron still earlier, for he is cited (on *Sat.* I. 8. 25) by Porphyrion. But the notes which we now have under the name of Acron were evidently put together by a writer who lived some time after the Roman Empire had adopted Christianity. These *scholia* are not of much assistance in the attempt to restore the words of Horace himself. Often they do not comment on the words in dispute and, when they do, Porphyrion often supports one reading, Acron the other. Sometimes, too, one reading is quoted as a heading to a note while the note itself explains the other. No editor has at present found the clue to all this tangle. Messrs Keller and Holder, who have examined far more MSS. than anybody else, have divided them into three classes, but the grounds on which they base this division are most unsatisfactory.

The chief editions of the text of Horace during the last 350 years are those of M. A. Muretus (Venice, 1551), D. Lambinus (Lyons, 1561), J. Cruquius (Antwerp, 1578), D. Heinsius (Leyden, 1605), T. Faber (Saumur, 1671), R. Bentley (Cambridge, 1711), C. Fea (Rome, 1811), F. Pottier (Paris, 1823), A. Meineke (Berlin, 1834), P. H. Peerlkamp (Haarlem, 1834), J. C. Orelli (Zurich, 1837), W. Dillenburger (Bonn, 1844), F. Ritter (Leipzig, 1856), K. Lehrs (Leipzig, 1859), H. A. J. Munro (Cambridge, 1869), O. Keller and A. Holder (ed. major, Leipzig, 1864—1870 and ed. minor, Leipzig, 1879). Among these, the edition of J. Cruquius is especially noteworthy because it is founded mainly on some MSS. (Blandinii) which formerly existed at Ghent (Blandenberg Abbey), but which were burnt in 1566 soon after Cruquius collated them. One of them, which editors call V (*vetustissimus*), was a very good MS., but not specially good in the odes. Fea used the MSS. now in Italy: Orelli those in Switzerland: Pottier those in Paris. Other editors have chosen MSS. in different libraries. Keller and Holder have inspected about 50 MSS. and have carefully collated about 25 in various countries.

The chief commentaries on Horace, at least in regard to the collection of illustrative matter, are those of Orelli and Dillenburger.

§ 8. *Imitations of Greek Poets.*

The following collection of fragments from Greek poets is taken from the edition of Horace by Keller and Häussner (Leipzig and Prague, 1885). It consists of passages which Horace seems to have imitated in thought or metre.

1. *C.* I. 1.—Pindari *frag.* 221 (ed. Bergk⁴).

. . 'Αελλοπόδων μέν τιν' εὐφραίνοισιν ἵππων
τίμια καὶ στέφανοι, τοὺς δ' ἐν πολυχρύσοις θαλάμοις βιοτά ·
τέρπεται δὲ καί τις ἔπι (φρασὶν) οἶδμ' ἐνάλιον
ναῒ θοᾷ σῶς διαστείβων . . .

2. *C.* I. 9.—Alcaei *fr.* 34.

῎Υει μὲν ὁ Ζεύς, ἐκ δ' ὀράνω μέγας
χείμων, πεπάγασιν δ' ὑδάτων ῥόαι.

— — — — —

— — — — —

κάββαλλε τὸν χείμων', ἐπὶ μὲν τίθεις
πῦρ, ἐν δὲ κίρναις οἶνον ἀφειδέως
μέλιχρον, αὐτὰρ ἀμφὶ κύρσᾳ
μάλθακον ἀμφι . . . γνόφαλλον.

3. *C.* I. 10.—Alcaei *fr.* 5.

Χαῖρε Κυλλάνας ὃ μέδεις, σὲ γάρ μοι
θῦμος ὑμνην, τοὶ κορύφαις ἐν αὔταις
Μαῖα γέννατο Κρονίδᾳ μίγεισα.

4. *C.* I. 12.—Pindari *Olymp.* 2. 1 sq.

'Αναξιφόρμιγγες ὕμνοι,
τίνα θεόν, τίν' ἥρωα, τίνα δ' ἄνδρα κελαδήσομεν;

5. *C.* I. 14.—Alcaei *fr.* 18.

'Ασυνέτημι τῶν ἀνέμων στάσιν ·
τὶ μὲν γὰρ ἔνθεν κῦμα κυλίνδεται,
τὸ δ' ἔνθεν · ἄμμες δ' ἂν τὸ μέσσον
ναῒ φορήμεθα σὺν μελαίνᾳ,
χείμωνι μοχθεῦντες μεγάλῳ μάλα ·
περ μὲν γὰρ ἄντλος ἱστοπέδαν ἔχει,
λαῖφος δὲ πᾶν ζάδηλον ἤδη
καὶ λάκιδες μέγαλαι κατ' αὐτο ·
χόλαισι δ' ἄγκοιναι.

6. *C.* I. 18.—Alcaei *fr.* 44.

Μηδὲν ἄλλο φυτεύσῃς πρότερον δένδριον ἀμπέλω.

7. *C.* I. 23.—Anacreontis *fr.* 51.

Ἀγανῶς οἷά τε νεβρὸν νεοθηλέα
γαλαθηνόν, ὅστ᾽ ἐν ὕλης κεροέσσης
ἀπολειφθεὶς ὑπὸ μητρὸς ἐπτοήθη.

8. *C.* I. 27, cf. III. 19. 9 sqq.—Anacreontis *fr.* 63.

Ἄγε δή, φέρ᾽ ἡμίν, ὦ παῖ,
κελέβην, ὅκως ἄμυστιν
προπίω, τὰ μὲν δέκ᾽ ἐγχέας
ὕδατος, τὰ πέντε δ᾽ οἴνου
κυάθους, ὡς ἀνυβριστί
ἀνὰ δηῦτε βασσαρήσω.

* *

ἄγε δηῦτε μηκέθ᾽ οὕτω
πατάγῳ τε κἀλαλητῷ
Σκυθικὴν πόσιν παρ᾽ οἴνῳ
μελετῶμεν, ἀλλὰ καλοῖς
ὑποπίνοντες ἐν ὕμνοις.

9. *C.* I. 34. 12 sqq.—Archilochi *fr.* 56.

Τοῖς θεοῖς τίθει τὰ πάντα· πολλάκις μὲν ἐκ κακῶν
ἄνδρας ὀρθοῦσιν μελαίνῃ κειμένους ἐπὶ χθονί,
πολλάκις δ᾽ ἀνατρέπουσι καὶ μάλ᾽ εὖ βεβηκότας
ὑπτίους κλίνουσ᾽ . . .

10. *C.* I. 37.—Alcaei *fr.* 20.

Νῦν χρὴ μεθύσθην καί τινα πρὸς βίαν
πώνην, ἐπειδὴ κάτθανε Μύρσιλος.

11. *C.* II. 2.—Comici cuiusdam versus a Plutarcho (περὶ δυσωπίας 10) servatus:

Οὐκ ἔστ᾽ ἐν ἄντροις λευκός, ὦ ξέν᾽, ἄργυρος.

12. *C.* II. 7. 9 sqq.—Archilochi *fr.* 6.

Ἀσπίδι μὲν Σαΐων τις ἀγάλλεται, ἣν παρὰ θάμνῳ
ἔντος ἀμώμητον κάλλιπον οὐκ ἐθέλων·
αὐτὸς δ᾽ ἐξέφυγον θανάτου τέλος· ἀσπὶς ἐκείνη
ἐρρέτω· ἐξαῦτις κτήσομαι οὐ κακίω.

13. *C.* II. 18.—Bacchylidis *fr.* 28.

Οὐ βοῶν πάρεστι σώματ᾽, οὔτε χρυσός, οὔτε πορφύρεοι τάπητες,
ἀλλὰ θυμὸς εὐμενής,
Μοῦσά τε γλυκεῖα καὶ Βοιωτίοισιν ἐν σκύφοισιν οἶνος ἡδύς.

14. *C.* III. 2. 13.—Tyrtaei *fr.* 10.

Τεθνάμεναι γὰρ καλὸν ἐπὶ προμάχοισι πεσόντα
ἄνδρ' ἀγαθὸν περὶ ᾗ πατρίδι μαρνάμενον.

15. *C.* III. 2. 14.—Simonidis *fr.* 65.

Ὁ δ' αὖ θάνατος κίχε καὶ τὸν φυγόμαχον.

16. *C.* III. 2. 25.—Simonidis *fr.* 66.

Ἔστι καὶ σιγᾶς ἀκίνδυνον γέρας.

17. *C.* III. 4.—Alcmanis *fr.* 45.

Μῶσ' ἄγε, Καλλιόπα, θύγατερ Διός,
ἄρχ' ἐρατῶν ἐπέων . . .

18. *C.* III. 11. 9 sqq.—Anacreontis *fr.* 75.

Πῶλε Θρῃκίη, τί δή με λοξὸν ὄμμασιν βλέπουσα
νηλεῶς φεύγεις, δοκέεις δέ μ' οὐδὲν εἰδέναι σοφόν;

* *
*

νῦν δὲ λειμῶνάς τε βόσκεαι κοῦφά τε σκιρτῶσα παίζεις
δεξιὸν γὰρ ἱπποσείρην οὐκ ἔχεις ἐπεμβάτην.

19. *C.* III. 12.—Alcaei *fr.* 59.

Ἔμε δείλαν, ἔμε πασᾶν κακοτάτων πεδέχοισαν.

20. *C.* IV. 3.—Hesiodi *theog.* 81 sqq.

Ὅντινα τιμήσωσι Διὸς κοῦραι μεγάλοιο
γεινόμενόν τε ἴδωσι διοτρεφέων βασιλήων,
τῷ μὲν ἐπὶ γλώσσῃ γλυκερὴν χείουσιν ἐέρσην,
τοῦ δ' ἔπε' ἐκ στόματος ῥεῖ μείλιχα . . .

21. *Epod.* 6. 13.—Archilochi *fr.* 94.

Πάτερ Λυκάμβα, ποῖον ἐφράσω τόδε;
τίς σὰς παρήειρε φρένας;
ἧς τὸ πρὶν ἠρήρησθα· νῦν δὲ δὴ πολύς
ἀστοῖσι φαίνεαι γέλως.

22. *Ep.* 13.—Anacreontis *fr.* 6.

Μεὶς μὲν δὴ Ποσιδηϊών
ἕστηκεν, νεφέλας δ' ὕδωρ
βαρύνει, Δία τ' ἄγριοι
χειμῶνες κατάγουσιν.

CARMINUM

LIBER QUARTUS.

———

I.

Intermissa, Venus, diu
    rursus bella moves? parce precor, precor.
non sum, qualis eram bonae
    sub regno Cinarae. desine, dulcium
mater saeva Cupidinum,   5
    circa lustra decem flectere mollibus
iam durum imperiis: abi,
    quo blandae iuvenum te revocant preces.
tempestivius in domum
    Pauli purpureis ales oloribus   10
comissabere Maximi,
    si torrere iecur quaeris idoneum:
namque et nobilis et decens
    et pro sollicitis non tacitus reis
et centum puer artium   15
    late signa feret militiae tuae,
et quandoque potentior
    largi muneribus riserit aemuli,

Albanos prope te lacus
　　ponet marmoream sub trabe citrea.   **20**
illic plurima naribus
　　duces tura, lyraeque et Berecyntiae
delectabere tibiae
　　mixtis carminibus non sine fistula;
illic bis pueri die   **25**
　　numen cum teneris virginibus tuum
laudantes pede candido
　　in morem Salium ter quatient humum.
me nec femina nec puer
　　iam nec spes animi credula mutui   **30**
nec certare iuvat mero
　　nec vincire novis tempora floribus.
sed cur heu, Ligurine, cur
　　manat rara meas lacrima per genas?
cur facunda parum decoro   **35**
　　inter verba cadit lingua silentio?
nocturnis ego somniis
　　iam captum teneo, iam volucrem sequor
te per gramina Martii
　　campi, te per aquas, dure, volubilis.   **40**

II.

Pindarum quisquis studet aemulari,
Iulle, ceratis ope Daedalea
nititur pinnis, vitreo daturus
　　nomina ponto.

I. 22, 23. Some edd. read *lyra—Berecynthia—tibia*; but almost
all MSS. are against them.

II. 2. The MSS. have *Iulle* or *Iule*. Many edd. believing *Iullus*
(or *Iulus*) *Antonius* to be an impossible name, read *ille*, a conjecture of

monte decurrens velut amnis, imbres 5
quem super notas aluere ripas,
fervet immensusque ruit profundo
    Pindarus ore,

laurea donandus Apollinari,
seu per audacis nova dithyrambos 10
verba devolvit numerisque fertur
    lege solutis,

seu deos regesve canit, deorum
sanguinem, per quos cecidere iusta
morte Centauri, cecidit tremendae 15
    flamma Chimaerae,

sive, quos Elea domum reducit
palma caelestis, pugilemve equumve
dicit et centum potiore signis
    munere donat; 20

flebili sponsae iuvenemve raptum
plorat et viris animumque moresque
aureos educit in astra nigroque
    invidet Orco.

multa Dircaeum levat aura cycnum, 25
tendit, Antoni, quotiens in altos
nubium tractus: ego apis Matinae
    more modoque

grata carpentis thyma per laborem
plurimum circa nemus uvidique 30
Tiburis ripas operosa parvus
    carmina fingo.

H. Peerlkamp (ob. 1865). But *Iullus* is now confirmed by in
scriptions (e.g. *C. I. L.* VI. no. 12010).

concines maiore poeta plectro
Caesarem, quandoque trahet ferocis
per sacrum clivum merita decorus   35
    fronde Sygambros :

quo nihil maius meliusve terris
fata donavere bonique divi
nec dabunt, quamvis redeant in aurum
    tempora priscum.   40

concines laetosque diés et urbis
publicum ludum super impetrato
fortis Augusti reditu forumque
    litibus orbum.

tum meae, siquid loquar audiendum,   45
vocis accedet bona pars, et 'o sol
pulcher, o laudande !' canam recepto
    Caesare felix.

'io'que dum procedis, 'io triumphe !'
non semel dicemus 'io triumphe !'   50
civitas omnis, dabimusque divis
    tura benignis.

te decem tauri totidemque vaccae,
me tener solvet vitulus, relicta
matre qui largis iuvenescit herbis   55
    in mea vota,

fronte curvatos imitatus ignis
tertium lunae referentis ortum,
qua notam duxit, niveus videri,
    cetera fulvus.   60

49. '*io*'*que* is my conjecture for *teque* of the MSS. Those edd. who
retain *teque* suppose that it refers to *Triumphe*, although *te* in l. 53
certainly refers to Antonius. The favorite emendation is *tuque*, but

III.

Quem tu, Melpomene, semel
    nascentem placido lumine videris,
illum non labor Isthmius
    clarabit pugilem, non equus impiger
curru ducet Achaico   5
    victorem, neque res bellica Deliis
ornatum foliis ducem,
    quod regum tumidas contuderit minas,
ostendet Capitolio ;
    sed quae Tibur aquae fertile praefluunt   10
et spissae nemorum comae
    fingent Aeolio carmine nobilem.
Romae, principis urbium,
    dignatur suboles inter amabilis
vatum ponere me choros,   15
    et iam dente minus mordeor invido.
o testudinis aureae
    dulcem quae strepitum, Pieri, temperas,
o mutis quoque piscibus
    donatura cycni, si libeat, sonum,   20
totum muneris hoc tui est,
    quod monstror digito praetereuntium
Romanae fidicen lyrae :
    quod spiro et placeo, si placeo, tuum est.

---

there is no occasion at all for the emphatic pronoun. *isque* and *atque*
have also been proposed. For '*io*'*que* cf. Ovid, *Trist.* IV. 2. 51, 52
tempora Phoebea lauro cingentur, '*io*'*que Miles* '*io*' *magna voce*
'*triumphe*' *canet*. Of course *io* (in *ioque*) is a monosyllable as in
Catullus LXI. (*io Hymen Hymenaee io*), on which see Munro, *Criticisms
and Elucidations*, p. 136, or Postgate, *Journ. Phil.* XVIII. p. 146.

IV.

Qualem ministrum fulminis alitem,
cui rex deorum regnum in avis vagas
   permisit expertus fidelem
      Iuppiter in Ganymede flavo,

olim iuventas et patrius vigor   5
nido laborum propulit inscium,
   vernique iam nimbis remotis
      insolitos docuere nisus

venti paventem, mox in ovilia
demisit hostem vividus impetus,   10
   nunc in reluctantis dracones
      egit amor dapis atque pugnae;

qualemve laetis caprea pascuis
intenta fulvae matris ab ubere
   iam lacte depulsum leonem   15
      dente novo peritura vidit:

videre Raeti bella sub Alpibus
Drusum gerentem Vindelici (quibus
   mos unde deductus per omne
      tempus Amazonia securi   20

IV. 17. Many edd. read *Raetis* (sc. *sub Alpibus*) a conjecture of
N. Heinsius (ob. 1681). Certainly Tacitus (*Hist.* I. 70, *Germ.* 1)
speaks of the *Raeticae Alpes*, and other writers distinguish the *Raeti* as
a different people from the *Vindelici*. But the MSS. and scholiasts here
are unanimous for *Raeti Vindelici* (cf. also Servius on *Aen.* I. 247); and
it would appear, from IV. 14. 7—14, that Hor. regarded *Vindelici* as a
generic name of various Alpine tribes, the Genauni, Breuni, Raeti etc.

dextras obarmet, quaerere distuli,
nec scire fas est omnia), sed diu
    lateque victrices catervae
      consiliis iuvenis revictae

sensere, quid mens rite, quid indoles   25
nutrita faustis sub penetralibus
    posset, quid Augusti paternus
      in pueros animus Nerones.

fortes creantur fortibus et bonis;
est in iuvencis, est in equis patrum   30
    virtus, neque imbellem feroces
      progenerant aquilae columbam:

doctrina sed vim promovet insitam,
rectique cultus pectora roborant;
    utcumque defecere mores,   35
      indecorant bene nata culpae.

quid debeas, o Roma, Neronibus,
testis Metaurum flumen et Hasdrubal
    devictus et pulcher fugatis
      ille dies Latio tenebris,   40

qui primus alma risit adorea,
dirus per urbes Afer ut Italas
    ceu flamma per taedas vel Eurus
      per Siculas equitavit undas.

post hoc secundis usque laboribus   45
Romana pubes crevit, et impio
    vastata Poenorum tumultu
      fana deos habuere rectos,

dixitque tandem perfidus Hannibal:
'cervi, luporum praeda rapacium,   50
   sectamur ultro, quos opimus
     fallere et effugere est triumphus.

gens, quae cremato fortis ab Ilio
iactata Tuscis aequoribus sacra
   natosque maturosque patres   55
     pertulit Ausonias ad urbes,

duris ut ilex tonsa bipennibus
nigrae feraci frondis in Algido,
   per damna, per caedes, ab ipso
     ducit opes animumque ferro.   60

non hydra secto corpore firmior
vinci dolentem crevit in Herculem,
   monstrumve submisere Colchi
     maius Echioniaeve Thebae.

merses profundo: pulchrior *exsilit*;   65
luctere: multa proruet integrum
   cum laude victorem geretque
     proelia coniugibus loquenda.

Carthagini iam non ego nuntios
mittam superbos: occidit, occidit   70
   spes omnis et fortuna nostri
     nominis Hasdrubale interempto.'

nil Claudiae non perficient manus,
quas et benigno numine Iuppiter
   defendit et curae sagaces   75
     expediunt per acuta belli.

---

65. Most MSS. have *evenit:* two only *exiet*. The reading *exsilit*
(or *exilit*) is from Rutilius Numatianus, a poet of the 5th cent.

V.

Divis orte bonis, optume Romulae
custos gentis, abes iam nimium diu;
maturum reditum pollicitus patrum
     sancto concilio, redi.

lucem redde tuae, dux bone, patriae: 5
instar veris enim vultus ubi tuus
affulsit populo, gratior it dies
     et soles melius nitent.

ut mater iuvenem, quem Notus invido
flatu Carpathii trans maris aequora   10
curictantem spatio longius annuo
     dulci distinet a domo,

votis ominibusque et precibus vocat,
curvo nec faciem litore dimovet:
sic desideriis icta fidelibus   15
     quaerit patria Caesarem.

tutus bos etenim rura perambulat,
nutrit rura Ceres almaque Faustitas,
pacatum volitant per mare navitae.
     culpari metuit fides,   20

nullis polluitur casta domus stupris,
mos et lex maculosum edomuit nefas,
laudantur simili prole puerperae,
     culpam poena premit comes.

v. 4. The MSS. mostly have *concilio* here, but *consilio* in III. 25. 6.
The latter is the more common designation of the senate.

quis Parthum paveat, quis gelidum Scythen,   25
quis Germania quos horrida parturit
fetus, incolumi Caesare? quis ferae
    bellum curet Hiberiae?

condit quisque diem collibus in suis
et vitem viduas ducit ad arbores;   30
hinc ad vina redit laetus et alteris
    te mensis adhibet deum;

te multa prece, te prosequitur mero
defuso pateris, et Laribus tuum
miscet numen, uti Graecia Castoris   35
    et magni memor Herculis.

'longas o utinam, dux bone, ferias
praestes Hesperiae!' dicimus integro
sicci mane die, dicimus uvidi,
    cum sol Oceano subest.   40

VI.

Dive, quem proles Niobea magnae
vindicem linguae Tityosque raptor
sensit et Troiae prope victor altae
    Phthius Achilles,

ceteris maior, tibi miles impar,   5
filius quamvis Thetidis marinae
Dardanas turris quateret tremenda
    cuspide pugnax.

ille, mordaci velut icta ferro
pinus aut impulsa cupressus Euro,   10
procidit late posuitque collum in
    pulvere Teucro.

ille non inclusus equo Minervae
sacra mentito male feriatos
Troas et laetam Priami choreis   15
    falleret aulam,

sed palam captis gravis, heu nefas heu,
nescios fari pueros Achivis
ureret flammis, etiam latentem
    matris in alvo,   20

ni tuis victus Venerisque gratae
vocibus divum pater adnuisset
rebus Aeneae potiore ductos
    alite muros.

doctor argutae fidicen Thaliae,   25
Phoebe, qui Xantho lavis amne crinis,
Dauniae defende decus Camenae,
    levis Agyieu.

spiritum Phoebus mihi, Phoebus artem
carminis nomenque dedit poetae.   30
virginum primae puerique claris
    patribus orti,

Deliae tutela deae, fugacis
lyncas et cervos cohibentis arcu,
Lesbium servate pedem meique   35
    pollicis ictum,

VI. 17. Many MSS. have *captis*, many omit the word altogether, and a few have *victor*. The authorities being doubtful, Prof. Housman proposes *cautis*, objecting to *captis* that to be 'stern to captives' is no proof of bravery. For *palam cautis* he compares *Aen.* I. 350 *clam ferro incautum superat*, and Ovid, *Metam.* XIII. 103, 104.

rite Latonae puerum canentes,
rite crescentem face Noctilucam,
prosperam frugum celeremque pronos
    volvere menses.   40

nupta iam dices : 'ego dis amicum,
saeculo festas referente luces,
reddidi carmen docilis modorum
    vatis Horati.'

VII.

Diffugere nives, redeunt iam gramina campis
    arboribusque comae ;
mutat terra vices et decrescentia ripas
    flumina praetereunt ;
Gratia cum Nymphis geminisque sororibus audet   5
    ducere nuda choros.
immortalia ne speres, monet annus et almum
    quae rapit hora diem.
frigora mitescunt Zephyris, ver proterit aestas
    interitura, simul   10
pomifer autumnus fruges effuderit, et mox
    bruma recurrit iners.
damna tamen celeres reparant caelestia lunae :
    nos, ubi decidimus,
quo pius Aeneas, quo Tullus dives et Ancus,   15
    pulvis et umbra sumus.
quis scit an adiciant hodiernae crastina summae
    tempora di superi ?
cuncta manus avidas fugient heredis, amico
    quae dederis animo.   20

cum semel occideris et de te splendida Minos
    fecerit arbitria,
non, Torquate, genus, non te facundia, non te
    restituet pietas:
infernis neque enim tenebris Diana pudicum   25
    liberat Hippolytum,
nec Lethaea valet Theseus abrumpere caro
    vincula Pirithoo.

VIII.

Donarem pateras grataque commodus,
Censorine, meis aera sodalibus.
donarem tripodas, praemia fortium
Graiorum, neque tu pessuma munerum
ferres, divite me scilicet artium,   5
quas aut Parrhasius protulit aut Scopas,
hic saxo, liquidis ille coloribus
sollers nunc hominem ponere, nunc deum.
sed non haec mihi vis, non tibi talium

VIII. Some editors reject this Ode altogether, but much of it is
Horatian in style, and there is a truly Horatian connexion between this
Ode and the next (cf. *Introd.* p. xxxii). But there can be little doubt
that some lines are interpolated. The following are the chief grounds
of suspicion: (1) The number of lines is not divisible by 4 (*Introd.*
p. xxvii): (2) in l. 17 the diaeresis (*Introd. ibid.*) is neglected in a very
singular manner: (3) in the same line, the burning of Carthage is
wrongly attributed to Scipio Africanus *Major:* (4) in l. 18 *eius* is
unparalleled save in an equally suspicious passage (III. 11. 18). Besides
this, there are many very doubtful expressions, e.g. *bonis ducibus,
lucratus, rediit, Calabrae Pierides, taciturnitas.* But the number of
lines to be rejected is obviously 2 or 6 or 10 or 14 (so as to leave a
remainder divisible by 4), and it is difficult to make these omissions.

res est aut animus deliciarum egens.　　　　10
gaudes carminibus : carmina possumus
donare et pretium dicere muneri.
non incisa notis marmora publicis,
[per quae spiritus et vita redit bonis
post mortem ducibus, non celeres fugae　　15
reiectaeque retrorsum Hannibalis minae,
non incendia Carthaginis impiae
eius, qui domita nomen ab Africa
lucratus rediit, clarius indicant
laudes, quam Calabrae Pierides; neque　　20
si chartae sileant, quod bene feceris,
mercedem tuleris. quid foret Iliae
Mavortisque puer, si taciturnitas
obstaret meritis invida Romuli ?
ereptum Stygiis fluctibus Aeacum　　　　25
virtus et favor et lingua potentium
vatum divitibus consecrat insulis.]
dignum laude virum Musa vetat mori.
caelo Musa beat : sic Iovis interest
optatis epulis impiger Hercules,　　　　30
clarum Tyndaridae sidus ab infimis
quassas eripiunt aequoribus rates,
ornatus viridi tempora pampino
Liber vota bonos ducit ad exitus.

If we reject only two lines (e.g. ll. 17 and 33), we leave *eius* and the
other suspicious expressions, and there is no complete passage of 6, 10
or 14 lines. The brackets in the text are so placed as to include every
considerable difficulty. If lines 14—27 are omitted, the sense will run
'It is not public inscriptions, but the Muse, that confers immortality.'
Many other suggestions have been made. The favorite remedy is to
omit ll. 15 *non*—19 *rediit* and also ll. 28 and 33. Unfortunately,
these latter lines are as well worth keeping as anything in the Ode.

IX.

Ne forte credas interitura, quae
longe sonantem natus ad Aufidum
    non ante vulgatas per artis
        verba loquor socianda chordis.

non, si priores Maeonius tenet 5
sedes Homerus, Pindaricae latent
    Ceaeque et Alcaei minaces
        Stesichorique graves camenae,

nec, siquid olim lusit Anacreon,
delevit aetas; spirat adhuc amor 10
    vivuntque commissi calores
        Aeoliae fidibus puellae.

non sola comptos arsit adulteri
crines et aurum vestibus illitum
    mirata regalisque cultus 15
        et comites Helene Lacaena,

primusve Teucer tela Cydonio
derexit arcu; non semel Ilios
    vexata; non pugnavit ingens
        Idomeneus Sthenelusve solus 20

dicenda Musis proelia; non ferox
Hector vel acer Deiphobus gravis
    excepit ictus pro pudicis
        coniugibus puerisque primus.

vixere fortes ante Agamemnona 25
muiti; sed omnes illacrimabiles
    urgentur ignotique longa
        nocte, carent quia vate sacro.

paulum sepultae distat inertiae
celata virtus.　non ego te meis　　　　　　　30
　　chartis inornatum silebo
　　　　totve tuos patiar labores

impune, Lolli, carpere lividas
obliviones.　est animus tibi
　　rerumque prudens et secundis　　　　　35
　　　　temporibus dubiisque rectus,

vindex avarae fraudis et abstinens
ducentis ad se cuncta pecuniae
　　consulque non unius anni,
　　　　sed quotiens bonus atque fidus　　40

iudex honestum praetulit utili,
reiecit alto dona nocentium
　　vultu, per obstantis catervas
　　　　explicuit sua victor arma.

non possidentem multa vocaveris　　　　45
recte beatum ; rectius occupat
　　nomen beati, qui deorum
　　　　muneribus sapienter uti

duramque callet pauperiem pati
peiusque leto flagitium timet,　　　　　50
　　non ille pro caris amicis
　　　　aut patria timidus perire.

IX. 31.　The MSS. are divided between *sileri* and *silebo.*

X.

O crudelis adhuc et Veneris muneribus potens,
insperata tuae cum veniet pluma superbiae
et, quae nunc umeris involitant, deciderint comae,
nunc et qui color est puniceae flore prior rosae,
mutatus, Ligurine, in faciem verterit hispidam,   5
dices 'heu,' quotiens te speculo videris alterum,
'quae mens est hodie, cur eadem non puero fuit,
vel cur his animis incolumes non redeunt genae?'

XI.

Est mihi nonum superantis annum
plenus Albani cadus ; est in horto,
Phylli, nectendis apium coronis ;
    est hederae vis

multa, qua crinis religata fulges ;   5
ridet argento domus ; ara castis
vincta verbenis avet immolato
    spargier agno ;

cuncta festinat manus, huc et illuc
cursitant mixtae pueris puellae ;   10
sordidum flammae trepidant rotantes
    vertice fumum.

ut tamen noris, quibus advoceris
gaudiis : Idus tibi sunt agendae,
qui dies mensem Veneris marinae   15
    findit Aprilem,

---

x. 2. Many emendations have been proposed for *pluma* : e.g.
poena, multa (i.e. punishment), *bruma, ruga.*

iure sollemnis mihi sanctiorque
paene natali proprio, quod ex hac
luce Maecenas meus affluentis
  ordinat annos.   20

Telephum, quem tu petis, occupavit
non tuae sortis iuvenem puella
dives et lasciva tenetque grata
  compede vinctum.

terret ambustus Phaethon avaras   25
spes, et exemplum grave praebet ales
Pegasus terrenum equitem gravatus
  Bellerophontem,

semper ut te digna sequare et ultra
quam licet sperare nefas putando   30
disparem vites. age iam, meorum
  finis amorum

(non enim posthac alia calebo
femina), condisce modos, amanda
voce quos reddas : minuentur atrae   35
  carmine curae.

XII.

Iam veris comites, quae mare temperant,
impellunt animae lintea Thraciae ;
iam nec prata rigent, nec fluvii strepunt
  hiberna nive turgidi.

nidum ponit, Ityn flebiliter gemens,   5
infelix avis et Cecropiae domus
aeternum opprobrium, quod male barbaras
  regum est ulta libidines.

dicunt in tenero gramine pinguium
custodes ovium carmina fistula 10
delectantque deum, cui pecus et nigri
    colles Arcadiae placent.

adduxere sitim tempora, Vergili;
sed pressum Calibus ducere Liberum
si gestis, iuvenum nobilium cliens, 15
    nardo vina merebere.

nardi parvus onyx eliciet cadum,
qui nunc Sulpiciis accubat horreis,
spes donare novas largus amaraque
    curarum eluere efficax. 20

ad quae si properas gaudia, cum tua
velox merce veni: non ego te meis
immunem meditor tinguere poculis,
    plena dives ut in domo.

verum pone moras et studium lucri, 25
nigrorumque memor, dum licet, ignium
misce stultitiam consiliis brevem:
    dulce est desipere in loco.

XIII.

Audivere, Lyce, di mea vota, di
audivere, Lyce: fis anus, et tamen
    vis formosa videri,
        ludisque et bibis impudens

et cantu tremulo pota Cupidinem   5
lentum sollicitas.   ille virentis et
  doctae psallere Chiae
   pulchris excubat in genis.

importunus enim transvolat aridas
quercus et refugit te quia luridi   10
  dentes te quia rugae
   turpant et capitis nives.

nec Coae referunt iam tibi purpurae
nec cari lapides tempora, quae semel
  notis condita fastis   15
   inclusit volucris dies.

quo fugit venus, heu, quove color? decens
quo motus? quid habes illius, illius,
  quae spirabat amores,
   quae me surpuerat mihi,   20

felix post Cinaram notaque *do*tium
gratarum facies? sed Cinarae brevis
  annos fata dederunt,
   servatura diu parem

cornicis vetulae temporibus Lycen,   25
possent ut iuvenes visere fervidi
  multo non sine risu
   dilapsam in cineres facem.

XIII. 21. *dotium* is an emendation by Prof. A. Palmer. The MSS.
have *notaque et artium*. Prof. Housman proposed *nota quot artium*,
but it is difficult to see what *artes* a lady's face could have. On the
other hand *dotes* (gifts, endowments) are frequently ascribed to a face or
figure. (See Lewis and Short, s.v. *dos*.)

XIV.

Quae cura patrum quaeve Quiritium
plenis honorum muneribus tuas,
    Auguste, virtutes in aevum
      per titulos memoresque fastus

aeternet, o qua sol habitabilis   5
illustrat oras, maxime principum?
    quem legis expertes Latinae
      Vindelici didicere nuper,

quid Marte posses. milite nam tuo
Drusus Genaunos, implacidum genus,   10
    Breunosque velocis et arces
      Alpibus impositas tremendis

deiecit acer plus vice simplici.
maior Neronum mox grave proelium
    commisit immanisque Raetos   15
      auspiciis pepulit secundis,

spectandus in certamine Martio,
devota morti pectora liberae
    quantis fatigaret ruinis,
      indomitas prope qualis undas   20

exercet Auster Pleiadum choro
scindente nubes, impiger hostium
    vexare turmas et frementem
      mittere equum medios per ignes.

XIV. 4. There is a great preponderance of authority here for *fastus*, though we had *fastis* in the previous ode (l. 15) and *fastos* in III. 17. 4.

sic tauriformis volvitur Aufidus,   25
qui regna Dauni praefluit Apuli,
   cum saevit horrendamque cultis
    diluviem meditatur agris,

ut barbarorum Claudius agmina
ferrata vasto diruit impetu,   30
   primosque et extremos metendo
    stravit humum, sine clade victor,

te copias, te consilium et tuos
praebente divos. nam tibi, quo die
   portus Alexandrea supplex   35
    et vacuam patefecit aulam,

fortuna lustro prospera tertio
belli secundos reddidit exitus,
   laudemque et optatum peractis
    imperiis decus arrogavit.   40

te Cantaber non ante domabilis
Medusque et Indus, te profugus Scythes
   miratur, o tutela praesens
    Italiae dominaeque Romae.

te fontium qui celat origines   45
Nilusque et Hister, te rapidus Tigris,
   te beluosus qui remotis
    obstrepit Oceanus Britannis,

---

28. The MSS. are divided between *meditatur* and *minitatur* and both these readings go back to the 4th century, for Servius quotes *meditatur* and Nonius *minitatur*.

te non paventis funera Galliae
duraeque tellus audit Hiberiae, 50
   te caede gaudentes Sygambri
     compositis venerantur armis.

XV.

Phoebus volentem proelia me loqui
victas et urbes increpuit lyra,
   ne parva Tyrrhenum per aequor
     vela darem. tua, Caesar, aetas

fruges et agris rettulit uberes 5
et signa nostro restituit Iovi
   derepta Parthorum superbis
     postibus et vacuum duellis

Ianum Quirini clausit et ordinem
rectum evaganti frena licentiae 10
   iniecit emovitque culpas
     et veteres revocavit artes,

per quas Latinum nomen et Italae
crevere vires famaque et imperi
   porrecta maiestas ad ortus 15
     solis ab Hesperio cubili.

custode rerum Caesare non furor
civilis aut vis exiget otium,
   non ira, quae procudit enses
     et miseras inimicat urbes. 20

non qui profundum Danuvium bibunt
edicta rumpent Iulia, non Getae,
   non Seres infidive Persae,
     non Tanain prope flumen orti.

nosque et profestis lucibus et sacris **25**
inter iocosi munera Liberi,
  cum prole matronisque nostris
   rite deos prius adprecati,

virtute functos more patrum duces
Lydis remixto carmine tibiis 30
  Troiamque et Anchisen et almae
   progeniem Veneris canemus.

CARMEN SAECULARE.

Phoebe silvarumque potens Diana,
lucidum caeli decus, o colendi
semper et culti, date quae precamur
    tempore sacro,

quo Sibyllini monuere versus   5
virgines lectas puerosque castos
dis, quibus septem placuere colles,
    dicere carmen.

alme Sol, curru nitido diem qui
promis et celas, aliusque et idem   10
nasceris, possis nihil urbe Roma
    visere maius !

rite maturos aperire partus
lenis, Ilithyia, tuere matres,
sive tu Lucina probas vocari   15
    seu Genitalis :

diva, producas subolem patrumque
prosperes decreta super iugandis
feminis prolisque novae feraci
    lege marita,   20

certus undenos deciens per annos
orbis ut cantus referatque ludos,
ter die claro totiensque grata
    nocte frequentis.

vosque veraces cecinisse, Parcae,   25
quod semel † dictum stabilis per aevum
Terminus servet, bona iam peractis
    iungite fata.

fertilis frugum pecorisque tellus
spicea donet Cererem corona ;   30
nutriant fetus et aquae salubres
    et Iovis aurae.

condito mitis placidusque telo
supplices audi pueros, Apollo ;
siderum regina bicornis, audi,   35
    Luna, puellas.

Roma si vestrum est opus Iliaeque
litus Etruscum tenuere turmae,
iussa pars mutare lares et urbem
    sospite cursu,   40

C. S. 26. The text is Bentley's emendation. The MSS. read *quod
semel dictum est stabilisque rerum | terminus servet.* The meaning of
this is most obscure, and it is incredible that Hor. permitted obscurity
in an ode intended to be sung publicly by a large chorus.

cui per ardentem sine fraude Troiam
castus Aeneas patriae superstes
liberum munivit iter, daturus
    plura relictis :

di, probos mores docili iuventae,   45
di, senectuti placidae quietem,
Romulae genti date remque prolemque
    et decus omne ;

quaeque vos bobus veneratur albis
clarus Anchisae Venerisque sanguis,   50
impetret, bellante prior, iacentem
    lenis in hostem.

iam mari terraque manus potentis
Medus Albanasque timet securis,
iam Scythae responsa petunt, superbi   55
    nuper, et Indi.

iam Fides et Pax et Honor Pudorque
priscus et neglecta redire Virtus
audet, apparetque beata pleno
    Copia cornu.   60

augur et fulgente decorus arcu
Phoebus acceptusque novem Camenis,
qui salutari levat arte fessos
    corporis artus,

si Palatinas videt aequus aras,   65
remque Romanam Latiumque felix
alterum in lustrum meliusque semper
    prorogat aevum.

quaeque Aventinum tenet Algidumque
quindecim Diana preces virorum   70
curat et votis puerorum amicas
    applicat auris.

haec Iovem sentire deosque cunctos
spem bonam certamque domum reporto,
doctus et Phoebi chorus et Dianae   75
    dicere laudes.

BOOK IV.

PRELIMINARY NOTE.

THE following summary of peculiarities in the composition of the Fourth Book is taken mainly from Orelli. In the 16 odes, eight different metres are employed. In the caesura of the Sapphic line and the diaeresis of the Alcaic, Horace has resumed the freedom which he avoided in the Third Book (see *Introd.* pp. xxviii, xxix). Elisions are more rare and a long vowel is nowhere elided except in I. 35. The initial syllables of the Alcaic stanza are always long. Hiatus between the lines is avoided and a short syllable is nowhere lengthened. There is a large number of words which Horace uses alone or for the first time: such are *faustitas, beluosus, tauriformis, domabilis, inimicare, apprecari, obarmare, remiscere, aeternare.* The uses of *spargier* also, and *surpuerat* and *ni* and *divum* (for *divorum*) and *quandoque* (I. 17) are unparalleled in the lyrics. The style is usually less terse than in the earlier works and is sometimes downright prosaic.

Ode I.

Scheme. Dost thou call me again to arms, Venus? Nay, spare me: I am not the man I was. Go rather to Paulus Maximus, the young, the beautiful, the brave. He, if he triumphs, will give thee fit reward. As for me, I am too old to love. And yet my tears, my stammering tongue, belie me, and all my thoughts are on Ligurinus.

The ode is placed first with a purpose. The nucleus of Book IV. consisted of the serious poems numbered 4 and 14. (See *Introd.* p. xiv.) But Horace has said several times (I. 6 and II. 12 are conspicuous instances) that his Muse was playful and not adapted to lofty themes, and he evidently preferred his lighter compositions to the more serious and dignified. By beginning the book with this ode, he 'put his best foot foremost.' See also the opening lines of the last Ode, 15. 1–4.

Metre. Third Asclepiad.

1. **intermissa** with *bella.* In III. 26 Horace had announced his intention to fight no more.

diu. If the dates generally given and adopted here (*Introd.* p. xviii) are right, there was an interval of 10 years (B.C. 23—13) between the publication of *C.* I.–III. and *C.* IV.

2. **bella moves,** 'are you taking the field?' Venus is the commander who calls upon Horace to bear arms in her service. For the expression cf. *Georg.* I. 509 *hinc movet Euphrates, illinc Germania bellum.*

4. **sub regno,** cf. III. 9. 9 *me nunc Thressa Chloe regit.*

Cinarae, probably a real person. She appears to have died young (IV. 13. 21, 22) and to have been very fond of Horace (*Epist.* I. 14. 33). Hence the epithet *bonae* 'kind.'

dulcium—saeva, a kind of oxymoron, implying that Horace likes to be in love but dislikes being forced to it.

5. **mater saeva Cupidinum,** repeated from I. 19. 1, where also he complains that Venus had obliged him *finitis animum reddere amoribus.*

6. **circa lustra decem** really means, as Kiessling remarks, ' *a man* of fifty.' *iam durum* of l. 7 agrees with this quasi-substantive, which is the object of *flectere.* Kiessling compares Ovid, *Metam.* I. 20 *pugnabant...sine pondere habentia pondus,* i.e. 'weighty things contended *with things without weight.*'

flectere, 'to twist and turn,' a metaphor from horse-taming. So *durum* seems to mean 'hard-mouthed.'

mollibus imperiis, probably dat. both with *durum* and *flectere = ad mollia imperia.* Cf. IV. 2. 56 *n.*

8. **revocant,** 'call thee back,' *re-* implying 'to thy duty.'

9. **in domum** with *comissabere* is an unusual expression, and some edd. would read *in domu.* Theocritus (3. 1) writes κωμάσδω ποτὶ τὰν Ἀμαρυλλίδα.

10. **Pauli.** Paulus Fabius Maximus was consul B.C. 11, when he was probably 33 years old. At this time (B.C. 15) he would be 29. He was a friend of Ovid who praises his eloquence (*Epp. ex P.* I. 2. 118 and II. 3. 75).

purpureis—oloribus, 'borne on the wings of thy lustrous swans.' For *purpureus,* 'dazzling' cf. *Aeneid* I. 590 *lumen iuventae purpureum.* For Venus' swans cf. III. 28. 15 *quae Cnidon—iunctis visit oloribus.*

11. **comissabere.** *comissor* is the Latin version of Gk. κωμάζω, as *tarpessita* for τραπεζίτης etc.

12. **idoneum,** cf. III. 26. 1.

13. **decens,** 'handsome,' as I. 4. 6 *Gratiae decentes.*

14. **reis,** cf. II. 1. 13 *insigne maestis praesidium reis.* Ovid also, addressing Paulus Maximus, speaks of *vox tua...auxilio trepidis quae solet esse reis.* To defend his clients in the law-courts was one of the chief duties of the *patronus.*

15. centum puer artium, gen. of description (Roby *L. G.* § 1308), cf. IV. 13. 21.

16. **militiae tuae,** cf. Ovid *Am.* I. 9. 1 *militat omnis amans et habet sua castra Cupido.*

17. **quandoque** = *quandocunque,* as in IV. 2. 34; cf. Roby *L. G.* § 2290.

18. **muneribus,** abl. of comparison with *potentior,* 'triumphant over the gifts of his lavish rival.'

19. **Albanos prope lacus.** Probably Paulus had a villa here. The two lakes Albanus and Nemorensis lie close together.

20. **te ponet marmoream,** 'he will set up thy statue in marble'; cf. Herodotus II. 41 οὗτος ἕστηκε λίθινος and *aeneus ut stes* in *Sat.* II. 3. 183.

citrea. The *citrus* is said to have been the African cedar, a sweet-smelling wood, otherwise called *thya* or *thyia.*

22. **duces,** of inhaling here, as of drinking in IV. 12. 4, cf. *traho.*

22, 23. **lyrae—tibiae** are doubtless gen. dependent on *carminibus,* cf. *Epod.* 9. 5 *sonante mixtum tibiis carmen lyra.* Orelli thinks *carminibus* means 'songs' and takes *lyrae* and *tibiae* as dat. with *mixtis:* but songs are mentioned afterwards, ll. 26, 27.

Berecyntiae tibiae. The Phrygian pipe, used in the worship of Cybele, was of a curved shape: *inflexo Berecyntia tibia cornu,* Ovid, *Fast.* IV. 181.

25. **bis die,** morning and evening.

28. **in morem Salium** for *in morem Saliarem,* as in I. 36. 12. The reference is to the dancing procession of the Salii, when they carried the *ancilia* round the city on March 1st and following days. (See *Salii* in Smith's *Dict. of Antiq.*)

ter, i.e. with a sort of polka-step, *tripudium,* cf. III. 18. 16.

30. **spes—mutui,** 'the fond hope of finding a heart to answer mine.' (Wickham.)

33. **cur,** 'Why,' if it is true that I can love no more.

34. **rara** seems to mean 'slow-dropping,' for the eyes of the aged cannot weep freely. It might mean 'unaccustomed.'

35. **parum decoro,** 'unbecoming.' The last syllable is hypermetric and is cut off before the vowel of *inter,* cf. IV. 2. 22, III. 29. 35, *Introd.* p. xxvi.

36. **cadit,** 'stops,' 'falters.'

38. **iam—iam** = *modo—modo.*

40. **aquas,** the Tiber. Horace sees the youth racing in the Campus or swimming in the river.

Ode II.

To C. Iullus Antonius, second son of M. Antonius the triumvir by Fulvia. He was educated by his stepmother Octavia, whose daughter Marcella he married. He was consul B.C. 10 and was in high favour with Augustus till B.C. 2, when he was put to death for an adulterous intrigue with Julia, Augustus's daughter. He is said to have been a poet and to have composed an epic, called *Diomedea*, in 12 books.

The allusions in ll. 32–36 show that the poem was written some time before the return of Augustus from Gaul in July B.C. 13. Possibly Antonius had asked Horace to celebrate this event in a Pindaric ode.

Scheme. To vie with Pindar, noblest of poets, is to court disaster and shame. He soars on high with swan-like pinions : I, like the busy bee, gather laboriously from flowers and groves my little store of poesy. It is for you, Antonius, to hymn the glories and virtues of Caesar on the day when he returns in triumph. I can but join in the cheering. From you, too, a noble sacrifice of thanksgiving will be due : mine must be a humbler offering.

Metre. Sapphic.

1. **Pindarum.** A great Theban poet, about B.C. 522—442. The only complete compositions of his that we have are a series of choral odes (ἐπινίκια) in praise of victors in the Greek athletic contests. Besides these, however, he wrote hymns to the gods, odes for processions (προσόδια), songs of maidens (παρθένεια), dancing-songs (ὑπορχήματα), drinking-songs (σκολιά), dirges (θρῆνοι) and encomia on princes. The following stanzas contain allusions to most of these styles of composition.

aemulari, 'rival,' not 'to imitate.'

2. **Iulle.** This spelling is attested by inscriptions, e.g. *C. I. L.* VI. 12010. The name *Iullus* or *Iulus* seems to be related to *Iulius* as *Tullus* to *Tullius.*

ceratis, 'fastened with wax.' The myth related that Daedalus made wings for his son Icarus and fastened them to his shoulders with wax, but that the youth soared so near the sun that the wax melted and he fell headlong into the Icarian sea. Cf. I. 3. 34.

ope Daedalea, 'by help of Daedalus.' For the adj. cf. *Herculeus labor* I. 3. 36.

3. **nititur,** cf. *Aeneid* IV. 252 *paribus nitens Cyllenius alis.*

4. **nomina,** for the plural cf. III. 27. 76.

ponto, i.e. the Icarian sea, the eastern part of the Aegaean. It was doubtless really so called from the island Icarus.

7, 8. **fervet—ore,** 'boils and rushes in a fathomless flood of words' (Wickham). *ore* in effect means 'outpour.'

10. **audacis** is explained by *nova verba* and *numeri lege soluti.* A dithyramb was a wild impassioned choral ode to Bacchus, accompanied by the Phrygian pipe.

nova verba, 'strange words.' Long compound words were especially appropriate to dithyrambs (Aristotle, *Poet.* 22. 14).

11. **numeris lege solutis**, 'wayward rhythms.' A dithyramb was not composed in a set form of scansion, which might be called the *lex* of the poem. For *numeri* cf. Cic. *Or.* 20. 67 *quidquid est enim quod sub aurium mensuram aliquam cadit, etiamsi abest a versu,—numerus vocatur, qui Graece ῥυθμός dicitur.*

13. **reges**, not the kings of Pindar's day but the demigod kings of the mythology, such as Pirithous who slew the Centaurs and Bellerophon who killed the Chimaera. The allusion is to Pindar's hymns and paeans.

14. **sanguinem**, 'offspring,' cf. III. 27. 65, *C. S.* 50.

17—19. The order is *sive dicit pugilemve equumve quos Elea palma d. r. caelestis.* The allusion is to the ἐπινίκια, the extant odes of Pindar. (A scheme of one is given in *Introd.* p. xix *n.*)

Elea palma. The palm-branch given to the victors in the Olympian games at Pisa in Elis.

18. **caelestis**, predicative. The palm brings them home exalted, cf. I. I. 5 *palmaque nobilis Terrarum dominos evehit ad deos.*

pugilemve equumve. The selection of boxing and chariot-racing (as in IV. 3. 4) was perhaps suggested by Pollux and Castor (*hunc equis, illum superare pugnis nobilem* I. 12. 26). In *equumve* the horse implies the charioteer; cf. Homer's ἵπποι τε καὶ ἀνέρες for 'charioteers and men on foot.'

19. **potiore signis.** For the idea cf. III. 30. 1 and IV. 8 (where it is expanded into a complete poem).

21. The *-ve* of *iuvenemve* is equivalent to *sive, si* being supplied from the previous stanza, cf. *Ars P.* 63, 64.

flebili = 'weeping,' 'tearful,' just as in II. 14. 6 *illacrimabilis* meant 'tearless,' 'unable to weep,' cf. *flebilis Ino* in *Ars P.* 123. The dative doubtless belongs to *plorat*: 'or if, for a weeping bride, he mourns her lover snatched away.' But *raptum sponsae* 'torn from his bride' is a possible construction.

22. **plorat.** The reference is to Pindar's θρῆνοι, dirges.

moresque. The last syllable is elided (*Introd.* p. xxvi).

23. **aureos**, predicative, like *caelestis* in l. 18. He extols them as golden, cf. IV. 3. 17 *n.*

nigroque. The last syllable is again elided. *nigro* is contrasted with *aureos.* Those golden virtues are too bright for gloomy Orcus.

25. **multa aura**, 'a full breeze,' lit. plenty of breeze. Pliny uses *multus sol* for 'plenty of sun.'

Dircaeum, from Dirce, a spring and streamlet near Thebes.

cycnum, cf. II. 20. 1-12, where Horace imagines himself a swan.

26. **Antoni.** This is the only place in which Horace uses a second form of address (after *Iulle* of l. 2). It is quite possible that he originally

began the ode at l. 25 and added ll. 1—24 afterwards. In any case, *concines* of l. 33 would be abrupt and obscure, unless some form of address had lately preceded.

27. **tractus**, 'expanses': cf. *caeli tractus* in *Aen.* III. 138.

apis. The comparison of poets to bees is common in Greek literature. Sophocles, for instance, was called 'Ἀτθὶς μέλισσα.

Matinae, Apulian, cf. I. 28. 3. Calabrian honey is praised in III. 16. 23.

28. **more modoque**, a formula common in Latin, like *Art und Weise* in German and 'shape or form' in English. It is practically a hendiadys for 'customary style.'

30. **plurimum**, doubtless with *laborem*, not with *nemus* as Bentley took it (meaning 'dense grove'). The contrast is between Pindar soaring easily on high and Horace working laboriously near the ground.

uvidi, cf. I. 7. 14, III. 29. 6.

31. **ripas**, absolutely, as in III. 25. 13.

32. **fingo**, 'build.' The verb would apply also to the construction of honeycombs.

33. **concines**. 'You shall sing to the lyre.' Lachmann's emendation *concinet* would be an improvement, for *concines* suggests that Horace is putting Antonius into that rivalry with Pindar which he has already declared to be absurd and impossible. But cf. I. 6 where Horace assigns to Varius a task which he declines himself on the ground that rivalry with Homer is impossible.

maiore plectro, probably abl. of description with *poeta* = 'poet of a mightier quill.' It may however be taken with *concines*. For *plectro* cf. II. 1. 40.

34. **quandoque** = *quandocunque* as in IV. 1. 17. The ode apparently was written some weeks before Caesar's return (July B.C. 13).

35. **per sacrum clivum**, 'down the sacred hill' i.e. the Via Sacra which descends a slope just before it reaches the Forum.

36. **fronde**, the laurel-wreath: but see the note on IV. 3. 7.

Sygambri, a tribe of N. Germany, between the Rhine and the Lippe. They crossed the Rhine and defeated M. Lollius in B.C. 16. Augustus, on receiving this news, set out for Gaul and stayed there three years.

37. **quo nihil maius** etc., cf. *Epist.* II. 1. 17 where the people praise Augustus *nil oriturum alias, nil ortum tale fatentes.*

39. **dabunt**: *donabunt* would be more usual, cf. *vis rapuit rapietque*, II. 13. 20, *colendi et culti, C. S.* 2. There is a slight difference between *dare* and *donare*: cf. Cic. *Verr.* IV. 16. 36 *multa aliis data atque donata.*

42. **ludum**, i.e. gladiatorial games.

impetrato, obtained by prayers. There are extant coins of B.C. 16 bearing the inscription *S. P. Q. R. V. S.* (vota suscepta) *PRO S.* (salute) *ET RED.* (reditu) *AVG.* There are also coins of B.C. 13 with the inscription *FORTVNAE REDVCI.*

44. litibus orbum, 'free from lawsuits,' owing to the holiday (*iustitium*). For the abl. cf. *vacuum duellis* IV. 15. 8.

45. siquid—audiendum, a *double entente* between 'if I can say anything worth hearing' and 'if I can make myself heard' amidst the cheers. Kiessling remarks on the comparative frequency of gerundives in the 4th Book (13 instances against 16 in the first three Books together). *loquar* is future.

46. bona pars, 'a large share,' as in *Sat.* I. 1. 61, *A. P.* 297.

sol, 'day.'

48. felix, i.e. fortunate in recovering Caesar.

49. ioque. See critical note. Edd. who read *tuque dum procedis* imagine that Antonius, being a member of Augustus' family, would ride in the procession. Those who read *teque dum procedis* imagine that the address is to the god Triumphus (cf. *Epod.* 9. 21), but this, as Bentley points out, involves some confusion, for the first *Io Triumphe* is the address of Horace himself, while the second is part of the cheering of the crowd.

52. tura. Temporary altars were set up along the route of the procession.

54. solvet, 'will release' from my vow undertaken *pro reditu Augusti.* For the comparison of Horace's offering with that of his richer friend cf. II. 17. 32.

55. iuvenescit, 'is growing.' The *vitulus* will soon be a *iuvencus*.

56. in mea vota, equivalent to a dative: cf. II. 8. 17 *pubes tibi crescit* 'grows for thy service.' Here *in mea vota* = for the payment of my vows.

58. referentis, bringing in due course: cf. II. 1. 28 *n.*

59. niveus videri, λευκὸς ὁρᾶσθαι (*Introd.* p. xxiii). The triviality of the last two stanzas is intentional and is imitated from Pindar, who likes a quiet close to a lofty ode: cf. the ending of III. 3 or III. 5 and *Introd.* p. xix.

Ode III.

To Melpomene, regarded here as the muse of lyric poetry. The ode, as Wickham remarks, bears some resemblance in general tenour to I. 1. 'There is the same division of the objects of Greek and Roman ambition, the same description of the poet's life and of his hope to be ranked with the Greek lyrists.'

Metre. Third Asclepiad.

1. Melpomene is usually regarded as the muse of tragedy, but Horace knows nothing of the special function of the Muses and appeals to Euterpe and Polyhymnia (I. 1. 32) or Clio (as I. 12. 2) or Melpomene (as here) indifferently.

semel, 'once for all' as I. 24. 16, *C. S.* 26.

3. **labor Isthmius,** i.e. at the Isthmian games, held every two years at Corinth.

4. **clarabit pugilem,** 'will make renowned as a boxer.'

5. **Achaico,** i.e. Greek, all Greece being included in the province of Achaia.

6. **res bellica,** 'the warrior's trade': cf. *res ludicra* 'the actor's trade,' *Epp.* II. 1. 180, and the title of Columella's book *de re rustica.*

Deliis foliis, laurels sacred to Delian Apollo. The triumphant general wore a crown of laurel and carried a laurel-branch in his hand. Kiessling contends that the tree of Delos *par excellence* was the palm (which certainly grew there) and that the allusion here and in IV. 2. 36 is to the palm-leaves embroidered on the triumphal tunic.

8. **contuderit,** fut. perf.

9. **Capitolio,** dat. A triumphal procession passed along the *Via Sacra* to the foot of the Capitol. The prisoners here turned aside, but the general went up to the temple of Jupiter Capitolinus.

10. **praefluunt** = *praeterfluunt.* So Verg. (*Aen.* VI. 705) uses *praenatat* for *praeternatat.* For the numerous watercourses at Tibur cf. I. 7. 13, 14.

12. **fingent—nobilem,** 'will mould him to win renown with Aeolian song.'

Aeolio, i.e. lyric, after Alcaeus and Sappho, who were Aeolian Greeks.

15. **vatum choros,** 'the choir of lyric poets,' alluding especially to the Greek canon of nine lyrists, viz. Pindar, Alcaeus, Sappho, Stesichorus, Ibycus, Bacchylides, Simonides, Alcman, Anacreon, cf. I. 1. 35.

16. **iam.** The publication of the first three Books and of the Carmen Saec. had made the difference. In II. 16. 40 and II. 20. 4 Horace speaks as if he suffered a good deal from *invidia.*

dente invido, 'the tooth of envy,' cf. *Sat.* I. 6. 46 *quem rodunt omnes libertino patre natum.*

17. **aureae.** The epithet is a convenient compendium for 'perfect, precious, rare': cf. *aureo plectro* II. 13. 26 and Pindar's address (*Pyth.* I. 1) to the χρυσέα φόρμιγξ of Apollo and the Muses.

18. **Pieri.** The Muses were called Pierides from Mt Pierus in Thessaly. The singular is unusual.

temperas, 'rulest': cf. *moderari fidem* in I. 24. 14.

20. **donatura,** 'able to give.' The part. = Gk. δοῦσα ἄν, and implies a condition: 'who canst give, if thou wilt.' *Septimi, Gades aditure mecum* in II. 6. 1 is somewhat similar.

cycni, for the singing of swans cf. II. 20. 10 *n.*

21. **muneris,** cf. Ovid *Trist.* I. 6. 6 *si quid adhuc ego sum, muneris omne tuist.*

22. **monstror,** cf. Persius I. 28 *at pulchrum est digito monstrari et dicier 'hic est.'*

23. **Romanae**, emphatic, like *Italos* (*ad modos*) in III. 30. 13.

24. **quod** is cognate object to *spiro* and *placeo*. 'The music that I breathe and the pleasure that I give (or 'the applause that I win') are thine.'

spiro = πνέω, to make music (properly on the flute): cf. II. 16. 38 *n.*, IV. 6. 29 and *Anth. Pal.* VII. no. 407 where Dioscorides speaks of Sappho as ἴσα πνείουσαν ἐκείναις (Πιερίσιν). Orelli, who gives this quotation, thinks *quod spiro* means 'the fact that I am inspired.'

Ode IV.

This ode was written, by command of Augustus (*Introd.* p. xiv), to celebrate the conquest of the Rhaeti by Nero Claudius Drusus in B.C. 15. Drusus was the son of Livia by her first marriage, younger brother of Tiberius and stepson of Augustus. He was father of Germanicus and of the Emperor Claudius. He was born B.C. 38 and died B.C. 9 in Germany. The campaign against the Rhaeti was conducted while Augustus was in Gaul. The Rhaeti occupied the Eastern Alps in the neighbourhood of Innspruck and Verona: the Vindelici dwelt to the north of them. (Horace regards the two peoples as one.) Drusus attacked from the south, while Tiberius, who was sent from Gaul by Augustus, advanced from the north.

Scheme. Like an eagle or a young lion, Drusus pounced on the Rhaeti. Their savage hordes succumbed to a man whom his blood and training had alike prepared for conquest. Romans, when you think of the Neros, remember the great day of the Metaurus and Hannibal's cry of despair.

Metre. Alcaic.

1. **qualem—alitem**. The accus. is governed by *propulit* and the other verbs of ll. 6–12. The simile is unusually awkward because parts of it (ll. 5–9), which are for the moment irrelevant, are inextricably complicated with the relevant part. In translation, a parenthesis must be made: 'Like the winged guardian of the thunderbolt, whom Juppiter, king of gods, made king of birds, because he found him trusty in the ravishing of fair-haired Ganymede:—aforetime youth and native vigour drove him forth from the nest to unknown labours' etc.

The protasis continues to l. 16: in effect *qualis aquila est vel leo, talem Rhaeti videre Drusum.*

ministrum fulm. Juppiter's eagle held a thunderbolt in his claws ready for the god to hurl. Hence Vergil *Aeneid* V. 255 calls him *Iovis armiger.*

alitem, adj. like *ales Pegasus* IV. 11. 26.

4. **in Ganymede**, 'in the matter of Ganymede' whom the eagle snatched from Troy to be Jove's cupbearer.

5. **olim iuventas** etc. The eagle's early progress is something like that of Drusus, but it is irrelevant to the present comparison, which is that of the eagle's swoop to Drusus' descent on the Rhaeti.

10. **vividus.** The repeated *v* (pronounced *w*) made this word a good epithet of swishing or whistling motion : cf. *vivida vis pervicit, venti vis verberat, fit via vi* and other examples collected by Munro *Lucr.* Introd. to Notes, Vol. II.³ p. 311.

13. **pascuis,** dat. with *intenta.*

14. **ab ubere.** No doubt, as Orelli says, *lacte depulsum* is one notion = ' weaned,'*ablactatum,* ἀπογαλακτισθέντα. Then *ab ubere* can be appended : 'just weaned from the teat of his tawny mother.' It happens however that *depellere a lacte, depellere ab ubere* and *depellere* alone are all used in Latin for 'to wean' (Vergil *Ecl.* 3. 82 : 7. 15 : *Georg.* III. 187). For the tautology, cf. Prop. I. 18. 15 *et tua flendo Turpia deiectis lumina sint lacrimis* and Ov. *Met.* I. 683 *euntem multa loquendo detinuit sermone diem.* It offends some editors here, who avoid it either by taking *ubere* as adj. with *lacte* ('rich milk'), or supposing that *fulvae m. ab ubere* refers to the roe-deer, which also, like the lion, is newly-weaned, or has wandered from its dam.

16. **vidit,** perfect, used of what often happens; cf. Roby §§ 1478, 1717.

17. **videre,** supply *talem.*

Raeti. See critical note.

18—22. **quibus—omnia.** This curious prosy parenthesis can be paralleled from Pindar and seems to be a deliberate imitation of him. Some edd. think it an interpolation and omit it, reading *et diu* for *sed diu* in l. 22. Orelli says that Horace is here scoffing at an absurd epic, called *Amazonis,* by Domitius Marsus, a contemporary poet. More probably it had been suggested to Horace that he might make a fine Pindaric myth about the connexion of the Amazons with the Vindelici but he found himself unequal to the feat.

20. **Amazonia securi,** called by Xenophon (*Anab.* IV. 4. 16) σάγαρις and said to have been a single-edged axe.

21. **quaerere distuli,** cf. *mitte sectari* I. 38. 2.

22. **diu lateque** with *victrices.*

24. **revictae,** 'conquered in their turn.'

25. **sensere,** 'have learnt to their cost.'

rite. The three words *rite, faustus* and *penetralia* have religious associations and imply that the Neros had been educated, as a Christian might say, 'in God's sight,' or 'before the Lord.'

mens, 'intellect': **indoles,** 'character.'

28. **Nerones.** Suetonius (*Tib.* I.) says that *Nero,* in the Sabine dialect, meant *fortis ac strenuus.*

29. **fortibus et bonis,** abl. cf. *edite regibus* I. I. I. In Latin the combined epithets *fortis et bonus,* like καλὸς κἀγαθός in Greek, are often used to describe a thorough gentleman: cf. *Epist.* I. 9. 13 *et fortem crede bonumque.* (Observe the contrast of *fortis* to καλός.)

33. **doctrina,** very emphatic: 'But it is training that brings out the innate force.' Cf. Cic. *pro Archia* 15 *cum ad naturam eximiam*

accesserit ratio quaedam conformatioque doctrinae, tum illud nescio quid praeclarum ac singulare solet existere.

35. **utcumque,** 'whenever': cf. I. 17. 10.

mores, i.e. morality, or good morals.

36. **bene nata**=τὰ εὐφυῆ, a neut. plur. used collectively, for 'scions of an honourable stock.' There is no occasion to supply *pectora* from l. 34.

38. **Metaurum flumen.** The name Metaurus is treated as an adj. : cf. *A. P.* 18 *flumen Rhenum.* The battle at the Metaurus occurred B.C. 207. Hasdrubal was marching southwards with reinforcements for Hannibal, who was in Lucania. M. Claudius Nero, the consul, leaving only a small detachment to watch Hannibal, secretly withdrew the best part of the Roman forces and hastened northwards against Hasdrubal, whom he utterly defeated at the Metaurus in Picenum.

39. **pulcher,** cf. *o sol pulcher* IV. 2. 46.

40. **Latio**=*Latinis,* dat. of person interested.

41. **qui primus.** The statement is an exaggeration. The first Roman victory in the 2nd Punic war was at Nola, B.C. 215.

adorea, 'glory.' The word is said to be derived from *ador* 'corn,' either because a largesse of corn was given to victorious soldiery, or because corn was regarded as the noblest possession : *gloriam—a farris honore adoream appellabant,* Pliny *N. H.* XVIII. 14. It would be imprudent to believe these etymologies. *alma* (lit. 'nourishing') appears to mean here 'refreshing,' as if the Romans recovered strength after their first victory.

42. **dirus.** Quintilian much admired this epithet of Hannibal: cf. II. 12. 2 *n.*

ut, 'ever since,' as in *Epod.* 7. 19.

43. **taedas,** 'pine woods.'

44. **equitavit,** 'galloped.' The verb is appropriate to Hannibal and used, by zeugma, of the rushing flame or wind. See III. 11. 42 *n.*

46. **crevit,** 'waxed ever stronger.'

impio, cf. Livy's story (XXVI. 11) of the plundering of the temple of Feronia.

47. **tumultu,** 'riot,' implying wanton outrage. The technical military sense of *tumultus,* viz. : 'insurrection' or 'civil war,' cannot apply here.

48. **rectos,** upright, i.e. restored after they had been knocked down by the ravagers.

51. **ultro,** literally, beyond what might be expected : 'we are actually *pursuing.*' So *Aeneid* IX. 126, 127 *at non audaci cessit fiducia Turno: Ultro animos tollit dictis atque increpat ultro.*

opimus, 'noblest,' used here in imitation of *spolia opima.*

54. **iactata** probably with *sacra,* not with *gens.*

57. **tonsa,** 'lopped.'

58. **frondis** with *feraci*, like *fertilis frugum*. (*Introd.* p. xxii.)

Algidus, a mountain in Latium covered with dark-green woods: cf. *nigris Erymanthi silvis* I. 21. 7.

61. **hydra.** The hydra's heads grew again immediately after Hercules had hacked them off. The comparison of the Roman army to the hydra appears to have been really made by Pyrrhus. *non* belongs to *firmior* and *maius*.

62. **vinci dolentem**, 'chafing at the foil,' Conington: for the infin. cf. *Introd.* p. xxiii.

63. **Colchi.** The allusion is to the armed men who sprang up when Jason, at Colchis, sowed the dragon's teeth.

64. **Echioniae Thebae.** Echion was the sole survivor of the warriors (σπαρτοί) who sprang from the dragon's teeth sown by Cadmus. He helped Cadmus to found Thebes. (In these comparisons Hannibal suggests that Rome has an inexhaustible supply of dragon's teeth from which she procured soldiers.)

65. **merses**=*si mersaris*. The object is *hanc gentem* supplied from l. 53.

profundo, possibly dative: cf. III. 16. 3 *domus demersa exitio* and *Introd.* p. xxiv.

pulchrior ought to mean 'all the *stronger.*' The text is probably corrupt here. See next note.

exsilit (or **exilit**). Editors who retain *evenit* suppose that it has its etymological meaning ('emerges'), but the verb almost always means 'to happen' or 'result.' Hence various critics have proposed *exilit, exiit* or *exiet* (an irregular future, which is supported by a few MSS.). Rutilius (about A.D. 420) read *exilit*, an appropriate word if the metaphor is taken from a cork, as in Pindar, *Pyth.* 11. 80. Dr Postgate compares Lucan VII. 248 *formidine mersā Prosilit...fiducia.* Cf. also *Epod.* 17. 52, *Sat.* 11. 6. 98.

66. **integrum victorem** means 'her victor as yet undefeated.' The intended sense is 'she, though often defeated, will at last throw her victor.'

67. **multa cum laude** must mean 'amidst loud applause' from the spectators. But the remark is most inappropriate. Hannibal could not think that the sympathies of the spectators were with Rome in the contest.

68. **proelia coniugibus loquenda.** This may be interpreted 'battles to be told of by Roman wives' or 'battles to be told of by Carthaginian widows.' The transition to battles, immediately after the suggestion of a wrestling match and a final victory, is very crude.

69. **nuntios superbos.** After Cannae, Hannibal sent to Carthage about a peck of gold rings taken from Roman knights.

70. **occidit, occidit.** For the pathetic repetition cf. II. 14. 1.

72. **nominis**, 'race,' as in *nomen Latinum* IV. 15. 13.

73—76. **nil Claudiae** etc. The last stanza is not part of Hannibal's speech, but a mild reflection of Horace himself, intended to bring the ode to a quiet close: cf. III. 3. 69-72.

75. **curae sagaces.** Some edd. think the allusion is to the sagacious care of Augustus, but the Neros deserved the compliment themselves (see l. 24). They had luck and they took pains.

76. **expediunt,** 'keep clear,' free from entanglement: cf. I. 27. 24 *illigatum—Pegasus expediet.*

acuta belli appears to mean 'the crises of war': on the analogy of 'acute' diseases (*acuta febris, ὀξὺς πυρετός*), which threaten immediate death: cf. *amara curarum* in IV. 12. 19.

Ode V.

To Augustus, during his absence in Gaul (B.C. 16—13: cf. introduction to the Second Ode).

Scheme. Return, Augustus: thou hast been too long away. When thou art here, the sun shines brighter, and as a mother yearns for her sailor son, so all Italy yearns for thee. To thee we owe security and plenty and purity and peace. All our happiness is of thy giving.

Metre. Fourth Asclepiad.

1. **divis bonis,** abl. abs. 'when the gods were kind': cf. *Sat.* II. 3. 8 *iratis natus dis.*

Romulae (for *Romuleae*): cf. *Dardanae genti* I. 15. 10 and *n.*

2. **custos,** cf. IV. 15. 17 *custode rerum gente.*

7. **it,** 'passes': cf. II. 14. 5 *quotquot eunt dies.*

9. **iuvenem,** governed by *vocat* of l. 13.

10. **Carpathii maris,** the sea between Crete and Asia Minor. The sailor-boy may be supposed to be in Rhodes or some neighbouring port. For the simile cf. III. 7. 1-5.

11. **spatio longius annuo,** 'longer than the regular season.' The *annuum spatium* is not a whole year, but the yearly sea-going period, from March to November. *longius,* of time, is not very common: cf. Caes. *B.G.* IV. 1. 7 *longius anno remanere.*

13. **votis—vocat,** cf. Livy I. 1 *cum bonis potius ominibus votisque et precationibus deorum dearumque libentius inciperemus.* Of course *ominibus* means 'consultation of the omens.'

17. **perambulat,** 'walks up and down' in ploughing.

18. **rura.** Bentley proposed *farra,* because *rura* is in the previous line. The repetition shows less than Horace's usual care—so does *dux bone* repeated in ll. 5 and 37.

Faustitas, an invention of Horace's, on the model of *Felicitas.*

19. **pacatum.** The reference is to the suppression of Sextus Pompeius and his piratical fleet, B.C. 36. Augustus himself says in the Monumentum Ancyranum *mare pacavi a praedonibus.*

20. **fides,** honesty. For *culpari metuit* cf. *metuente solvi* II. 2. 7.

22. **mos et lex**, cf. III. 24. 35 where Horace asks *quid leges sine moribus Vanae proficiunt?* The law alluded to here is the *lex Iulia de adulteriis* of B.C. 18.

23. **simili prole**, abl. abs. 'the children being like their fathers,' cf. Hesiod, *Works and Days*, 235 τίκτουσιν δὲ γυναῖκες ἐοικότα τέκνα γονεῦσιν.

24. **premit**, 'checks,' 'represses.'

25. **Parthum.** The Parthians surrendered the standards of Crassus in B.C. 20.

Scythen. The Sauromatae were driven across the Danube B.C. 16.

26. **Germania—fetus**, alluding to the Sygambri. See introduction to Ode 2.

28. **Hiberiae.** The Cantabri, after many years of turbulence, were finally subdued by Agrippa B.C. 19.

29. **condit diem**, 'sees the sun down,' Wickham: cf. Verg. *Ecl.* 9. 52 *cantando condere soles* and Callimachus' ἥέλιον λέσχῃ κατεδύσαμεν. The point is that every man can work undisturbed the whole day long in his vineyard.

collibus, 'vineyards,' which are usually laid out on a hillside: cf. *Formiani colles* I. 20. 12.

30. **ducit**, 'weds.' *viduas*, 'widower,' for the vine was regarded as the wife, the tree on which it was trained as the husband, cf. *Epod.* 2. 9 *adulta vitium propagine Altas maritat populos* and *platanus caelebs* in II. 15. 4.

31. **vina.** For the plur. cf. I. 11. 6, III. 21. 8.

alteris mensis, cf. *mensae secundae*, Verg. *Georg.* II. 101, where Conington says 'drinking did not begin till after the first course, when it was commenced by a libation (*Aeneid* I. 723 etc.).'

32. **adhibet**, 'invites your presence': cf. *Aeneid* V. 62 *adhibete Penates—epulis.* Dion Cassius (LI. 19) says that, in B.C. 24, the senate decreed that libations should be poured to Augustus in private, as well as public, banquets.

34. **tuum numen**, i.e. the *Genius Augusti.*

35. **Castoris—Herculis.** The genitives are required by *memor* but are also dependent on *numen*, the full construction being *uti Graecia* (*miscet numen*) *Castoris et Herculis.*

37. **dux bone**, cf. supra l. 18 *n.*

longas ferias, an ingenious way of suggesting 'May thy reign be a long one.'

38. **integro die**, abl. abs. 'when the day is unbroken,' i.e. in our morning prayers.

39. **sicci**, cf. I. 18. 3.

uvidi, 'when we have well drunken,' cf. II. 19. 18.

Ode VI.

This ode is obviously a prelude to the *Carmen Saeculare*, which was written for the Ludi Saeculares of B.C. 17. The poet claims here, for the larger composition, the assistance of Apollo, and the attention of the chorus.

Scheme. Apollo, who punishest a boastful tongue,—it was thy doing that Achilles fell and Aeneas was preserved from slaughter to found Rome—maintain now the honour of Italian poesy. Ye girls and boys, mark my beat when you sing the praises of Apollo and Diana. Hereafter, you will be proud to remember that you sang my ode at the secular festival.

Metre. Sapphic.

1. **magnae vindicem linguae**, 'punisher of a boastful tongue.' This aspect of Apollo seems to be emphasized in order to emphasize, by implication, the modesty of Horace. The poet's first thought, when he was asked to compose a *Carmen Saeculare*, was to ask for the aid of Apollo. *magna lingua* is a translation of μεγάλη γλῶσσα.

proles Niobea. Niobe, who had six sons and six daughters, boasted of her superiority to Latona, who had only two children. For this insolence, Latona's children, Apollo and Diana, slew Niobe's children. The story is told in *Iliad* XXIV. 602.

2. **Tityos** was a giant who offered outrage to Latona and was also slain by Apollo and Diana: cf. especially III. 4. 77 and *Odyssey* XI. 576.

3. **sensit**, 'found to his cost': cf. IV. 4. 25.

prope with *victor*, 'almost victorious,' cf. Cic. *Fam.* I. 4. 1 *paene amicus.* Achilles slew Hector but was himself slain, before the capture of Troy, by Apollo (so Soph. *Philoct.* 334) or by Paris with the aid of Apollo (according to Hector's prophecy in *Iliad* XXII. 358).

4. **Phthius.** Achilles' home was at Phthia in Thessaly.

5—24. These five stanzas are parenthetic. The invocation is resumed at l. 25.

tibi impar, 'no match for thee': cf. *Aeneid* I. 475 *infelix puer atque impar congressus Achilli.* In the same sense *dispar* in I. 17. 25.

6. **filius Thetidis**, 'as the son of sea-born Thetis' and therefore a demigod.

7. **Dardanas**, for *Dardanias*, cf. IV. 5. 1 *Romulae gentis.*

8. **cuspide** with *quateret*. The spear of Achilles is described by Homer (*Il.* XIX. 388) as βριθὺ μέγα στιβαρόν· τὸ μὲν οὐ δύνατ' ἄλλος 'Αχαιῶν Πάλλειν κ.τ.λ. *quateret*=Homer's ἐλέλιξεν, 'made them quake.'

pugnax, 'eager for battle,' III. 3. 27. (Some edd. connect *cuspide pugnax* : cf. Livy XXII. 37 *pugnaces missili telo gentes.*)

11. **late**, 'sprawling huge.' So in *Odyssey* XXIV. 39 the ghost of Agamemnon says to the ghost of Achilles σὺ δ' ἐν στροφάλιγγι κονίης κεῖσο μέγας μεγαλωστί.

13. **ille.** The repeated pronoun, as Wickham says, marks the

contrast between 'what *was* and what *might have* been if Apollo had not interfered.'

equo, perhaps dat. =*in equum*, cf. *Introd*. p. xxiv.

14. **Min. sacra mentito**, 'that feigned Minerva's worship' (Wickham). The wooden horse, by means of which Troy was taken, was represented to be a gift to Pallas in place of the stolen Palladium: cf. *Aeneid* II. 17 and 183.

male feriatos, 'making untimely holiday.'

16. **falleret**=*fefellisset*, as *ureret* in l. 19=*ussisset*, the protasis being *ni...pater adnuisset* of l. 22, which means, in effect, 'if Achilles had lived to capture Troy.'

The imperfect subj. suggests the indic. *ille non fallebat...sed urebat* (Roby *L. G.* § 1470), with the sense 'He would not have been for stealing unawares on the Trojans...but would have been for burning' etc.

aulam, 'the court,' for 'the courtiers.'

17. **palam captis**, 'taken in open fight.' These words, so emphatically placed, convey the real antithesis to *non falleret* as much as if Hor. had written *sed palam caperet et gravis ureret* etc. For *palam* cf. Cic. *Or.* 12. 38 *non ex insidiis sed aperte ac palam*. **gravis**, 'pitiless.'

18. **nescios fari**=*infantes*.

19. **etiam latentem** etc., 'the babe unborn.' So Agamemnon, in *Iliad* VI. 57 says of the Trojans τῶν μήτις ὑπεκφύγοι αἰπὺν ὄλεθρον χεῖράς θ' ἡμετέρας, μηδ' ὅντινα γαστέρι μήτηρ κοῦρον ἐόντα φέροι.

21. **ni**. This form is used by Horace in lyrics only here and in *Epod.* 1. 8. *ni*=*si non*, cf. II. 17. 28.

22. **divum**, gen. plur. This form also is used by Horace only here and perhaps in I. 2. 25 (where it may be accus. sing.). Lucian Müller thinks the whole stanza an interpolation, partly because of these oddities of expression and partly because the reason here implied for the death of Achilles (viz. Apollo's wish to save Aeneas), seems inconsistent with that given in the first stanza.

23. **rebus Aeneae**, 'the fortunes of Aeneas': cf. *Aeneid* VIII. 471 *res Troiae*.

potiore alite, 'with a better omen': cf. I. 15. 5 *mala avi*.

ductos, 'traced,' cf. *Aeneid* I. 423 *pars ducere muros*.

25. **argutae**, 'clear-voiced,' λιγείας, as in III. 14. 21.

26. **Xantho**, not the Trojan river (also called Scamander), but a river of Lycia near Patara, where Apollo had a famous shrine (cf. III. 26. 10). A similar turn is given to a description of Apollo in III. 4. 61 *qui rore puro Castaliae lavit Crinis solutos*. The long hair of the god, like his beardless chin (*levis*, l. 28), is a sign of perpetual youth.

27. 'Uphold the glory of the Italian muse.' *Dauniae* perhaps means 'Apulian' (cf. III. 30. 10), for Horace was born in Apulia, but more probably it means only 'Italian' (as in II. 1. 34) and Horace is simply asking Apollo to show the same favour to an Italian poet which

he had often shown to the Greeks. (Hence Bentley in l. 25 read *Argivae* with some inferior MSS. for *argutae*.) It is quite possible that some literary men of the time had suggested that a Greek poet should be employed to write the *Carmen Saeculare*.

28. **Agyieu**, 'god of streets,' a Greek name for the sun-god. In Oriental cities the blazing heat of the roadways is especially noticeable.

29. **spiritum**, 'music': cf. II. 16. 38 and IV. 3. 24.

31. **virginum** etc. The *Carmen Saec*. was written for a chorus of 27 maidens and 27 boys.

33. **tutela,** used collectively for 'wards.' Artemis was the protectress of children (κουροτρόφος, φιλομεῖραξ, παιδοτρόφος are titles given to her in various parts of Greece), cf. Catullus XXXV. 1 *Dianae sumus in fide Puellae et pueri integri*.

34. **cohibentis**, 'stopping.'

35. **servate** = *observate*, 'watch the Lesbian measure and the stroke of my thumb.' The Lesbian measure is the rhythm of the Sapphic stanza: the thumb-stroke on the lyre seems to mean the leading notes of the tune.

37. **rite**, 'with due worship,' cf. IV. 15. 28 *rite deos prius adprecati*.

Latonae puerum. So Bacchus is called *Semeles puer* in I. 19. 2.

38. **crescentem face.** 'with her crescent light' (Wickham). For the abl. cf. IV. 4. 46 *secundis laboribus crevit*.

Noctilucam, the moon-goddess Diana.

39. **prosperam frugum,** 'who gives prosperity to our crops': cf. *fertilis frugum, Carm. S.* 29 and *Introd.* p. xxii.

celerem volvere, cf. *Introd.* p. xxiii.

pronos, 'swiftly moving,' cf. *A. P.* 60 *proni anni*.

41. **nupta.** The poet addresses one of the maidens. 'Some day when you are a wife' (Wickham).

42. **luces** = *dies*, cf. *profestis lucibus* IV. 15. 25.

43. **reddidi,** 'rendered,' used of repeating what has been taught, as in IV. 11. 35.

docilis = *docta,* cf. *Introd.* p. xxiv. For the gen. *modorum* cf. I. 15. 24 *sciens pugnae*.

Ode VII.

To Torquatus, doubtless the same person to whom *Epist.* I. 5 is addressed. Nothing is known of him except that he was an orator (cf. l. 23) and that a speech of his, in defence of one Moschus of Pergamum, accused of poisoning, was extant in Porphyrio's time.

Scheme. Spring is returning and the changing seasons remind us that life too is fleeting. But for us there is no returning after death. Let us therefore enjoy ourselves while we may, since there is no appeal from the tribunal of Minos (cf. I. 4).

Metre. The First Archilochian, not used by Horace elsewhere. The lines are scanned as follows:

1, 3. $-\simeq|-\simeq|-,\simeq|-\underset{\smile}{\smile}|-\smile|-\underline{\smile}$

2, 4. $-\smile\smile|-\smile\smile|\simeq.$

Technically described, these lines are a dactylic hexameter, followed by a dactylic trimeter catalectic.

3. **mutat vices,** 'is passing through her regular changes.' The accus. is cognate.

4. **praetereunt ripas,** 'flow past their banks,' instead of overflowing them.

5. **Gratia cum geminis sororibus,** in effect, the three Graces: cf. III. 19. 16 and I. 4. 6.

7. **almum diem,** 'the genial day,' cf. *Aeneid* V. 64 *si nona diem mortalibus almum Aurora extulerit.*

8. **hora,** 'time as it flies,' as in II. 16. 32.

9. **Zephyris,** abl. instrum., cf. Verg. *Georg.* I. 44 *Zephyro putris se glaeba resolvit.*

proterit, 'tramples on' as it advances: III. 5. 34.

10. **simul**=*simul ac.*

11. **effuderit,** 'has poured' from the *cornu copiae*: cf. I. 17. 15.

12. **iners,** 'sluggish,' when work is at a standstill. Cf. *Georg.* I. 299 *hiems ignava colono.*

13. **damna caelestia** seems to mean 'losses *caused by* the sky' (i.e. by the winter-season). In *Georg.* IV. 1 *aerii mellis caelestia dona* is somewhat similar (see Conington's note). *lunae* obviously means 'months.'

14. **decidimus,** sc. *de vita,* cf. *Epist.* II. 1. 36 *scriptor abhinc annos centum qui decidit.*

15. **quo,** sc. *deciderunt.*

Tullus dives. Livy (I. 31) says *devictis Sabinis, cum in magna gloria magnisque opibus regnum Tulli ac tota res Romana esset* etc. But the epithet here is strange and unnecessary, and as the MSS. vary between *dives Tullus* and *Tullus dives,* possibly the text has been tampered with. In *Epist.* I. 6. 27 Horace says simply *ire tamen restat Numa quo devenit et Ancus.*

16. **pulvis et umbra,** cf. Sophocles *Electra* 1158 ἀντὶ φιλτάτης Μορφῆς σποδόν τε καὶ σκιὰν ἀνωφελῆ.

17. **adiciant**=*adiecturi sint:* cf. II. 4. 13, 14.

hodiernae summae, 'our total as it stands to-day': cf. *vitae summa brevis* I. 4. 15.

19. **heredis,** cf. *Sat.* II. 3. 151 *avidus iam haec auferet haeres.* Horace elsewhere, e.g. II. 3. 20, II. 14. 25, speaks of heirs with a certain jealousy, natural in a childless man.

amico animo, imitated from φίλῃ ψυχῇ 'your own dear soul.'

21. **Minos**, one of the judges of Hades. (The others were Rhadamanthus and Aeacus, II. 13. 22.)

splendida arbitria, 'his august decision.' The epithet is frequently applied to oratory and probably refers here to Minos' stately eloquence. It may, however, mean 'clear-voiced.'

23. **genus**, 'noble birth': cf. I. 14. 13.

25. **tenebris**, with *liberat*, abl. of separation.

pudicum Hippolytum, an example of *pietas*, for the chaste Hippolytus was a votary of Artemis (Diana). A different legend related that Hippolytus *was* restored to life by Aesculapius (*Aeneid* VII. 765, Ovid *Met.* XV. 479).

27. **Theseus**. The point lies in *caro*. Love too is powerless to restore the dead. The example is suggested by the mention of Hippolytus, who was the son of Theseus; but Hor. ignores the legend that Theseus, though he could not rescue Pirithous from Hades, was himself rescued by Heracles.

Ode VIII.

To C. Marcius Censorinus, who was consul B.C. 8 and died A.D. 2. He was of so obliging a disposition that Velleius Paterculus (II. 102) calls him *vir demerendis hominibus natus.*

Scheme. I would gladly give my friends choice works of art, if I had them, and to you, Censorinus, I would give the best of any. But I have them not nor do you require them. You love poetry and poetry is mine to give. Note well the value of it. Poetry, better than monuments or titles, can confer immortality and can exalt a hero to heaven.

So many objections can be justly taken to ll. 13–24 that it is impossible to think they are authentic. Two lines more (see critical note) are probably also to be excised, though it is difficult to select two. The remainder of the ode is unworthy of Horace, but some critics find faults enough to prove that it could not have been written by a Roman at all. Yet it has been included in Hor.'s works since the 2nd century.

Metre. First Asclepiad.

1. **donarem.** The protasis (*si possem*) can be supplied from l. 5 *divite me artium* etc.

commodus, 'obliging.' The sense is reinforced by *grata* 'delightful.'

2. **meis** seems to have some emphasis, as if Horace wished to say *et ego donarem.* Possibly Censorinus had sent Horace a work of art for a New Year's present. It was the custom at Rome to exchange presents (*strenae*) at the Saturnalia (in December) and on the Kalends of March. (The dat. *sodalibus* depends on *donarem.*)

aera, 'bronze bowls,' λέβητες, or other vases, ornamented with chasing and repoussé work. Such vessels were largely produced in Corinth; hence *Ephyreia aera* in *Georg.* II. 464: cf. *Sat.* II. 3. 21 and see *Dict. of Antiq. s. v. caelatura.*

3. **tripodas.** See *Dict. of Antiq. s. v.* A tripod was a very

common prize in Greek athletic contests: cf. Pindar *Isthm.* I. 18, Herod. I. 144, *Aeneid* V. 110.

4. **neque tu pessuma**, a litotes for *et tu optima*.

5. **ferres**=*acciperes*: cf. III. 16. 22 *ab dis plura feret*.

divite me, 'were I rich.' **scilicet**, 'that is to say' (a very unusual sense).

artium, 'works of art': cf. *Epist.* I. 6. 17 *aeraque et artes Suspice*, and *Aeneid* V. 359 *clypeum—Didymaonis artes*.

6. **Parrhasius.** An Ephesian painter who lived at Athens about B.C. 410. He was the rival of Zeuxis.

Scopas of Paros, a celebrated sculptor who flourished about B.C. 380—350. Many of his works were in Rome, e.g. the statue of Apollo which Augustus set up in his great Palatine temple. The famous statue of Demeter seated, now in the British Museum, is attributed to him or his younger contemporary Praxiteles.

7. **liquidis**, in contrast with *saxo*.

8. **sollers ponere**, cf. *callidus condere* I. 10. 7 and *Introd.* p. xxiii.

ponere, 'to portray': cf. *A. P.* 34 of a sculptor who can do portions of a figure, but *ponere totum Nesciet*.

9. **haec vis**=*haec copia*, 'this abundance of works of art': cf. IV. 11. 4 *n.*

10. **res**, 'fortune.' Censorinus was too rich to require such presents.

animus, 'tastes.'

deliciarum, 'dainty delights,' often applied to works of art.

12. **muneri.** For the dat. cf. *Sat.* II. 3. 23 *callidus huic signo ponebam milia centum*.

13. The worst passage begins here. It will be seen, from the following notes, how many faulty expressions it contains.

notis publicis. For the abl. cf. Livy VI. 29 *tabula litteris incisa*. The reference is to the *titulus* inscribed on a statue, recording the exploits of the person portrayed: cf. Ovid *Trist.* III. 3. 72 *quosque legat versus oculo properante viator, Grandibus in tituli marmore caede notis.*

14. **bonis ducibus.** The epithet is utterly prosaic. (Contrast the genuine *dux bone* of IV. 5. 5 and 37.) The addition of *post mortem*, too, in l. 15 is mere padding, to fill out the lines. *retrorsum* of l. 16 perhaps has some point, meaning that Hannibal's threats were hurled back at his own head.

17. **non incendia** etc. The absence of *caesura* is suspicious (for I. 18. 16 and II. 12. 25 are not quite parallel). But, besides this, the line contains a bad blunder in history, for the Scipio Africanus (Major) who defeated Hannibal and was a friend of Ennius, was not the Scipio Africanus (Minor) who burnt Carthage. It is true that poets, like other people, may make mistakes in history, e.g. Keats thought that

Cortes discovered the Pacific, and Spenser confused Lionel Duke of Clarence (son of Edward III.) with George (brother of Edward IV.). But the conquest of Carthage was as important in Roman history as the conquest of the Armada in English history and it is inconceivable that Horace made a mistake about it or that the mistake, being made, was not pointed out to him and corrected.

18. **eius.** The pronoun *is* is rarely used by Augustan poets at all and does not occur elsewhere in the odes except in III. 11. 18, a passage otherwise suspicious. *illius* would be used here even in prose.

19. **lucratus** again is a rare and somewhat vulgar word, generally having the sense of 'pocketing' Its use here is quite unparalleled. For the sense cf. *Sat.* II. 1. 65 *Laelius aut qui Duxit ab oppressa meritum Carthagine nomen.*

20. **Calabrae Pierides.** The allusion is to the Muse of Ennius, who was a native of Rudiae in Calabria and wrote, in his *Annales*, a poetical account of the Second Punic War. But the combination of *Calabrae* with *Pierides* (a local name from Mount Pierus in Thessaly) is absurd. *Ceae Camenae* of IV. 9. 7 is different, for *Camenae* is not a local name.

21. **si chartae sileant.** *chartae* are properly sheets of papyrus. The word is often used for the 'writings,' as we might say the 'pages,' of an author (cf. IV. 9. 30). But *chartae*, for 'books' in general, is a rare and apparently contemptuous expression (cf. *Epist.* II. 1. 35). The verb *sileant* is also remarkable, for it is an exceptional compliment, worthy of an exceptional metaphor, when we say of a page that 'it speaks.' Thus Catullus (LXVIII. 46) specially begs the Muses *facite haec charta loquatur anus.* With *silere* we expect a *personal* nominative, as in IV. 9. 30 *non ego te meis Chartis inornatum silebo.*

22. **Iliae Mavortisque puer.** The mention of both parents is unusual (cf. IV. 6. 37), but Wickham sees some point in it ('despite his royal and divine ancestry'). The legend that Ilia, daughter of Aeneas (not Rhea Sylvia), was mother of Romulus is followed in I. 2. 17. It seems to have been of Greek origin and was certainly popularised by Naevius and Ennius.

23. **taciturnitas** is an odd personification of Silence, cf. *lividas obliviones* in IV. 9. 32.

24. **meritis** seems to be intended for 'deserts,' but in Augustan Latin it almost invariably means 'services' (cf. III. 30. 15, *Epist.* II. 1. 10). The natural interpretation of the passage is: 'if Silence stood in the way of the services of Romulus' (i.e. prevented them from reaching our ears). This might pass, but the addition of *Romuli* (after the already redundant *Iliae Mavortisque puer*) is most suspicious.

25. **Aeacum.** Perhaps a mistake for Rhadamanthus, who, in Homeric mythology, ruled the isles of the blest (*Od.* IV. 564). Everywhere else (e.g. II. 13. 22, Ovid *Met.* XIII. 25) Aeacus is represented as one of the judges of Hades, far removed from the islands of the blest. It is true that, by omitting the line, we deprive *consecrat* of an accusative: but *beat*, just below, is also without an accusative.

G. H. IV. **4**

26. virtus with *vatum*: 'the commanding force and favour and eloquence of mighty poets,' cf. Cic. *de Or.* II. 27. 120 *oratoris vis illa divina virtusque.* (Some editors think the *virtus* is that of Aeacus, but Horace has just said, in the previous ode, ll. 21–24, that nobody can be saved from death by his own *virtus.*)

potentium, cf. III. 30. 12 *ex humili potens.*

27. divitibus insulis (abl. loc.), 'the islands of the blest,' as in *Epod.* 16. 42. These islands, the μακάρων νῆσοι, were supposed to lie in the Atlantic, far to the West of the world. Homer intends the same place by the name of the Elysian plain (*Od.* IV. 563). Hither favoured heroes were translated, without dying. (In later mythology, the Elysian fields were supposed to be a part of Hades, where the ghosts of the pious were allowed to dwell.)

consecrat, 'immortalizes': cf. *sacrare* I. 26. 11. (For the singular verb cf. I. 3. 3.)

28. In IV. 9. 25–28 Horace says that many great men have failed to obtain the notice of the Muse.

29. caelo—beat. 'The Muse can bestow the bliss of heaven.' The illustrations which follow occur also in III. 3. 9–16. Horace does not go quite so far as Ovid who says (*ex Ponto* IV. 8. 55) *di quoque carminibus, si fas est dicere, fiunt,* which means, in effect, that there would be no gods if poets had not made them.

sic, i.e. by the good offices of the Muse.

30. optatis epulis. Kiessling, who regards the ode as a sort of comic Christmas card, thinks the allusion is to the Herakles of Greek comedy, who is always represented as a huge feeder (e.g. in the *Birds* of Aristophanes). For *epulis* cf. III. 3. 11, 12.

31. clarum sidus, in apposition with *Tyndaridae,* Castor and Pollux. Cf. I. 3. 2 *n.,* I. 12. 27.

33. ornatus—pampino. Almost the same words occur in III. 25. 20, but there are many examples of such repetition in Horace (e.g. IV. 1. 5).

34. vota, 'prayers.' Liber stands for Bacchus, who was not a god by birth, his mother Semele being a mortal, cf. III. 3. 13 *n.*

Ode IX.

To M. Lollius, whose cognomen is unknown, though he was a very distinguished man. He was consul B.C. 21 and though, in B.C. 16, he suffered a heavy defeat from the Sygambri, Augustus does not seem to have withdrawn his confidence from him. At any rate, he was appointed in B.C. 2 special guardian and adviser to C. Caesar (son of Agrippa and Julia and grandson to Augustus). Tiberius afterwards said that he abused his trust (Tac. *Ann.* III. 48) and both Pliny and Velleius give a very bad account of him as a greedy and licentious hypocrite. The eulogy which Horace bestows on him in this ode may have been composed early in his career, but it must have required some courage to publish it so soon after B.C. 16.

Scheme. Think not, Lollius, that my lyrics will not be immortal. Homer indeed holds the first place, but Pindar and Simonides and the whole choir of Greek lyrists are still remembered. Many a hero has failed of his just reward for want of a poet to renown him. I will therefore not omit you from my pages. Your wise and virtuous mind is a supreme authority and example not for one year merely but always while you do your duty fearlessly. It is not wealth that brings happiness but self-command and honesty and affection and patriotism.

Metre. Alcaic.

1. **ne forte credas.** The addition of *forte* renders it clear that this is a final clause and not a prohibition. 'Lest you should think, as perhaps you might...(remember that) Pindar and Simonides are still famous.' Wickham quotes *Epist.* I. 1. 13 *Ac ne forte roges quo me duce, quo lare, tuter: Nullius addictus iurare in verba magistri Quo me cunque rapit tempestas, deferor hospes* (cf. also *Sat.* II. 1. 80, *Epist.* II. 1. 208). It is not however to be supposed that a prohibition would require *ne credideris.* See the note on *Albi, ne doleas* I. 33. 1.

2. **longe sonantem,** cf. III. 30. 10, IV. 14. 25.

natus ad Aufidum. The Aufidus is the chief river of Apulia, but Venusia is not very near the main stream. Here, as in III. 30, Horace mentions his humble provincial birthplace with pride.

3. **non ante vulgatas,** 'never before made known' in Italy: cf. *Epist.* I. 19. 32 *hunc (Alcaeum) ego, non alio dictum prius ore, Latinus Vulgavi fidicen.*

4. **verba socianda chordis,** i.e. lyric poems.

5. **si,** concessive (=*etsi*). See Lewis and Short s.v. I. B. 5.

Maeonius. Smyrna and Colophon, both in Maeonia (i.e. Lydia), claimed, among other towns, to be the birthplace of Homer. The poet is often called *Maeonides,* as if *Maeon* was his father's name.

6. **latent,** 'are forgotten.'

7. **Ceae camenae,** i.e. the Muse of Simonides of Ceos: cf. II. 1. 38.

minaces, 'warlike,' cf. II. 13. 31.

8. **graves,** 'stately.' Stesichorus, of Himera in Sicily (circa B.C. 630), was regarded by the ancients as the nearest akin to Homer of all the lyrists.

9. **lusit,** of sportive song, as in I. 32. 2.

10. **spirat,** 'breathes music,' cf. IV. 3. 24.

11. **commissi** = 'confided,' as a secret.

calores, 'passion': cf. *calere,* 'to be in love' I. 4. 19.

12. **puellae,** gen. with *fidibus.*

13. **non sola.** Horace passes, as Wickham says, 'from tne defence of lyric poetry...to the power of verse generally.' Poetry, even lyric poetry, can be immortal. Nay, it confers immortality.

comptos crines. The accus. depends on *mirata.* 'Spartan Helen

4—2

was not the only woman who was ever fired with love through admiration of the braided locks of her seducer' etc. It is true that *arsit* might govern an accus. (as Verg. *Ecl.* 2. 1 *Corydon ardebat Alexin*), but the construction would be awkward here and Horace elsewhere uses the abl. with *ardere* (II. 4. 9 *arsit virgine* and III. 9. 5). For *mirari* of admiration leading to love cf. I. 4. 19, *Epod.* 3. 10.

14. **crines.** The charms of a fine head of hair, beautifully kept, are often mentioned in classical literature: cf. I. 15. 14 and see the article *coma* in Smith's *Dict. of Antiq.*

illitum, literally 'painted on,' but the reference is to designs embroidered in gold thread: cf. *Aeneid* III. 483 *picturatas auri subtemine vestes.* Eurip. *Orest.* 840 χρυσεοπήνητα φάρεα.

15. **cultus,** 'his princely ways': cf. *feros cultus* I. 10. 2.

16. **comites,** 'his suite.'

17. **Cydonio,** i.e. Cretan, from Cydon a town in Crete: cf. *calami spicula Gnosii* I. 15. 17.

18. **non semel,** in effect 'many a Troy was ravaged.' As Kiessling remarks, there are two series of examples introduced in nearly the same terms: *non sola—primus—non semel*: *non solus—non primus—multi* (cf. the series of *nec—aut* in II. 9. 1—17). Observe the emphatic position of these leading words.

20. **Idomeneus Sthenelusve.** Here, as in I. 15, Horace chooses the less famous heroes of the Trojan war.

21. **dicenda Musis proelia,** cf. *proelia coniugibus loquenda* IV. 4. 68.

22. **Deiphobus** was Hector's brother. His chief exploits are recounted in *Iliad* XII. and XIII.

26. **illacrimabiles,** 'unwept': cf. *flebilis* I. 24. 9. But *illacrimabilis*= 'unable to weep' in II. 14. 6.

27. **urgentur,** cf. I. 24. 5.

28. **sacro.** The poet is *musarum sacerdos* (III. 1. 3) and is under the protection of Apollo, Bacchus and Mercury. The epithet here has some suggestion of an *active* meaning: the *sacer vates* is one who can *sacrare, consecrare* ('immortalize' IV. 8. 27 *n.*). For the thought cf. Pindar *Nem.* VII. 12 ταὶ μεγάλαι γὰρ ἀλκαὶ σκότον πολὺν ὕμνων ἔχοντι δεόμεναι: and Tac. *Agr.* 46 *multos veterum velut inglorios et ignobiles oblivio obruet.*

29. **sepultae** and **celata** as Wickham says, belong in thought both to *inertiae* and to *virtus.* 'Once in the grave, valour differs little from cowardice, if they be unrecorded': cf. II. 15. 18 *n.*, *Epod.* 5. 37.

inertiae dat., cf. *differt sermoni* in *Sat.* I. 4. 48.

31. **chartis** with *inornatum*, not with *silebo*: 'I will not leave you unadorned with a poem of mine.' *inornatum* is proleptic: 'I will not be silent about you, so that you are unadorned.' Lollius was already *ornatus*, 'distinguished.'

33. **impune**, 'unresisted.'

carpere, with the tooth of envy: as in Cic. *pro Balb.* 26 *maledico dente carpere*: cf. IV. 3. 16.

lividas, cf. *taciturnitas invida* IV. 8. 23.

34. **obliviones**, personified: 'powers of oblivion.' The plur. was perhaps suggested by the use of *oblivia* in the plural.

35. **rerum prudens**, 'versed in affairs': cf. Nepos *Con.* I. 2 *prudens rei militaris.*

36. **dubiis**, 'dangerous,' 'critical': cf. Tac. *Ann.* I. 64 *secundarum ambiguarumque rerum sciens.*

rectus, 'well-balanced.'

37. **vindex**, 'prompt to punish greed and wrong in others and proof itself against the universal temptation' (Wickham).

abstinens pecuniae. For the gen. cf. *sceleris purus* I. 22. 1 and *Introd.* p. xxii.

39. **consulque**. Grammatically, *consul* (like *vindex*) is yet another description of the *animus* of Lollius, and Bentley shows, by a long array of passages, that *animus* is often combined, in Latin, with nouns that involve a verbal notion (e.g. *Aeneid* IX. 205 *animus lucis contemptor*, Juvenal XIII. 195 *animus tortor*, and so also *animus liberator, carnifex* etc.). The popular etymology of *consul* was *qui recte consulit* (Varro *L. L.* V. 80).

40. **sed quotiens** etc. The asyndeton (i.e. absence of conjunctions) of *praetulit, reiecit, explicuit* shows that these verbs are coordinate and have the same subject. The subject must be *animus*, but Horace speaks as if the subject were Lollius himself and not his mind. 'You have a mind...that is consul not for one year only, but whenever it (i.e. you), acting as an upright and honest judge, prefers duty to advantage or rejects with lofty mien the bribes of the guilty or carries its arms victorious through the hordes of the enemy.' In effect, 'your mind is consul so long as you do your duty fearlessly.' Lollius had been consul once and Horace means to say that he did not lose a jot of his dignity when his year of office expired: cf. III. 2. 17 *virtus repulsae nescia sordidae Intaminatis fulget honoribus Nec sumit aut ponit securis Arbitrio popularis aurae.* It was a Stoic doctrine that the wise and virtuous man is *rex*, though he wears no crown (cf. *Sat.* I. 3. 125, *Epist.* I. 1. 106).

41. **honestum**, τὸ καλόν, 'honourable conduct,' 'duty.'

43. **catervas**. This is a metaphor for the throng of wicked men or wicked desires whereby the integrity of a judge is assailed.

44. **explicuit**: cf. *expediunt* IV. 4. 76.

46. **beatum**, cf. II. 2. 16–24 and *Epist.* I. 16. 20 *neve putes alium sapiente bonoque beatum.*

The doctrine here belongs practically to all the Greek schools of philosophy alike.

51. **ille.** For the repetition of the subject cf. I. 9. 16 *nec dulces amores Sperne puer neque tu choreas.*

Ode X.

To Ligurinus, a pretty spoilt boy (cf. IV. I. 33).

Metre. Second Asclepiad.

1. **Veneris muneribus**, cf. *Iliad* III. 54 δῶρ' Ἀφροδίτης, ἥ τε κόμη τό τε εἶδος.

2. **insperata**, 'unexpected.'

pluma, 'down,' cf. πτίλον.

superbiae, dat. with *veniet*.

3. **involitant.** For the long hair of petted boys cf. II. 5. 21, III. 20. 14.

deciderint, 'shall have been cut off.' In Greece, boys at the age of puberty cut off their long locks and offered them as a sacrifice to some god.

5. **verterit**, 'shall have turned' (i.e. changed): cf. Livy V. 49. 5 *iam verterat fortuna.*

6. **alterum**, 'so different.'

8. **his animis**, dat. with *redeunt*, 'to the feelings that I have now.'

Ode XI.

An invitation to Phyllis to attend a feast which the poet is preparing to celebrate Maecenas' birthday, April 13th. This is the only mention of Maecenas in the IVth Book (cf. *Introd.* p. xiv).

Metre. Sapphic.

2. **Albani**, a good Italian wine, rather strong. In *Sat.* II. 8. 16 the host, Nasidienus, offers it as an alternative to Falernian.

3. **apium**, 'parsley,' used in winter instead of flowers, I. 36. 16, II. 7. 24.

nectendis coronis, dat.

4. **vis**=*copia*. This use is very common in Cicero, e.g. *Tusc.* V. 32. 91 *vis auri argentique.*

5. **qua** with *fulges*, for *crinis religata* means ' wearing your hair tied back in a knot': cf. I. 5. 4, II. 11. 23. Some edd. take *qua* with *religata* as if the hair was tied with ivy. *qua fulges*='with which you look so pretty.'

6. **ridet**, 'is gay': cf. Catull. LXIV. 284 *quo permulsa domus iucundo risit odore.*

ara, no doubt an altar of turf: cf. I. 19. 13 *hic vivum mihi caespitem, hic Verbenas, pueri, ponite* etc.

7. **verbenis**, 'greenery,' boughs of myrtle, laurel, olive etc.: any *frondes sacratae* according to Servius (on *Aen.* XII. 120). *castis,* 'holy,' i.e. permitted by ritual: cf. *Aen.* VII. 71 *castis adolet altaria taedis.*

8. **spargier**=*spargi.* This archaic form is not used elsewhere in

the lyrics, but occurs five times in the Satires and Epistles (*laudarier*, *sectarier* etc.). It seems therefore to belong to the language of familiar conversation, like *avet* and *cursitant*.

9. **manus**, the household of slaves. *puellae* is not often used for maidservants: but cf. *Epist.* I. 5. 7.

11. **flammae**, the kitchen-fire.

12. **vertice**, 'whirling the smoke in a coil.'

13. **ut noris**, 'in order that you may know,' a final clause, like *ne forte credas* IV. 9. 1.

14. **gaudiis**, dat. = *in gaudia*.

15. **Veneris marinae**, patroness of Phœnician sailors, III. 26. 5. Ovid (*Fasti* IV. 25–30) says that Romulus, mindful of his own descent, assigned the first month of the year to Mars, the second to Venus.

16. **findit**, ' divides' : the word *Idus* being connected etymologically with *dividere*.

19. **affluentis—annos**, 'counts the increase of his years.'

21. **Telephum**, mentioned in I. 13 and III. 19.

petis, III. 19. 27.

22. **non tuae sortis** with *iuvenem*, 'a youth above your sphere': cf. *disparem* l. 31.

27. **gravatus** = *indignatus*, 'ill-brooking' (Wickham).

29. **te digna**, 'things meet for you.'

30. **putando**, 'by thinking it wrong to nurse illicit hopes.'

33. **calebo** with abl. ('to be in love with') as I. 4. 19 (*Lycidan*) *quo calet iuventus Nunc omnis, et mox virgines tepebunt.*

34. **condisce**, 'come and learn.'

35. **reddas**, cf. IV. 6. 43.

Ode XII.

An invitation to one Vergilius, not the poet, who died B.C. 19, but a merchant (see l. 25) who was a frequent visitor in the houses of rich young men.

Scheme. The spring is come: the swallows are building and the shepherds piping to their flocks. The time invites the flowing bowl, Vergilius: but if you want to drink wine with me, you must pay scot and lot with a box of spikenard. Come, bring your ware and let your business go hang. We will be merry for once.

Metre. Fourth Asclepiad.

1. **temperant**, 'calm' after the winter storms. The usual sense is 'rule,' 'control' (I. 12. 16, III. 4. 45).

2. **animae Thraciae**. These opening lines seem to be imitated from a Greek poet, to whom a Thracian breeze was *westerly*: cf. *Iliad* IX. 5 Βορέης καὶ Ζέφυρος, τώ τε Θρήκηθεν ἄητον. Horace usually speaks of the zephyr as the companion of spring (I. 4. 1, IV. 7. 9 and *Epist.* I. 7.

1 3 *cum zephyris et hirundine prima*) and of the Thracian wind as very violent (I. 25. 11, *Epod.* 13. 3).

3. **prata—turgidi.** Horace was never in the country at this time of year and had forgotten what it looked like. Spring is just the time when rivers are swollen.

6. **infelix avis,** the swallow. According to the mythology, Procne, daughter of Pandion, king of Athens (hence *Cecropiae domus*) and sister of Philomela, was married to Tereus, king of Thrace. In revenge for an outrage done by him to her sister, Procne slew her son Itys and served up his flesh to her husband. The rest of the story is told in different ways, but Roman poets usually say that Procne was changed into a swallow, Philomela into a nightingale (Verg. *Georg.* IV. 15, Ovid *Met.* VI. 412), while Greeks often call Philomela the swallow, Procne the nightingale.

et. The addition of *et* is awkward, for *aeternum opprobrium* seems to be nom. and properly in apposition to *infelix avis.* The only alternative is to take *opprobrium* as accus. to *gemens* and refer *ulta est* to *Cecropia domus*: 'she mourns Itys and the reproach of Cecrops' house, in that it cruelly punished' etc. But to ascribe the crime, as well as the reproach, to Cecrops' house seems unwarranted.

For *opprobrium* cf. *oppr. pagi* II. 13. 4.

7. **male** with *ulta est*: 'cruelly.'

barbaras, the epithet belongs properly to *regum* (cf. *Introd.* p. xxiv): 'outrages of barbarian kings.'

9. **dicunt**: cf. *dic age tibia* III. 4. 1.

pinguium. The epithet is surprising, for obviously the sheep have only lately been let out of the fold.

11. **deum cui** etc. Pan, *ovium custos* as Vergil calls him (*Georg.* I. 17).

nigri: clothed in dark foliage: cf. I. 21. 7.

14. **pressum Calibus,** cf. *prelo domitam Caleno* I. 20. 9.

ducere, 'quaff': I. 17. 22.

16. **nardo—merebere.** 'You shall earn your wine with spikenard.' The guest was to bring nard in exchange for the wine: cf. I. 31. 12 *vina Syra reparata merce* and III. 19 (introductory note).

17. **onyx,** a box made of spar or alabaster. The contrast of the little scent-box with the huge *cadus* is meant to be comic. Nard was very expensive. The box of nard with which Mary anointed our Saviour's feet (John xii. 3) was worth 300 *denarii*, about £12 of our money.

18. **Sulpiciis horreis,** 'the stores of Sulpicius.' Porphyrio says that they belonged to Sulpicius Galba and that the *horrea Galbae* still existed in his day and were still stored with comestibles.

accubat, 'leans against the wall.'

19. **largus donare.** For the infin. cf. *Introd.* p. xxiii.

amara curarum, i.e. bitter cares: cf. *A.P.* 49 *abdita rerum*, *Sat.* II. 8. 83 *ficta rerum*: and see Munro's note on *strata viarum* Lucr. I. 315.

20. **eluere**, cf. III. 12. 2 *mala vino lavere.*

22. **merce**, 'your ware,' i.e. the box of nard.

23. **immunem**, 'scot-free,' ἀσύμβολον, i.e. bringing no contribution. See III. 23. 17 *n.*

24. **plena**, cf. II. 12. 24 *plenas Arabum domos.*

25. **verum** is used only here in the Odes.

pone = *depone*, 'put away.'

studium lucri. Dillenburger, who thought Vergil the poet was addressed, explained this to refer to haggling over the unfair bargain that Horace proposes, viz. expensive nard for comparatively cheap wine.

26. **nigrorum,** the gloomy fires of death: cf. *Aen.* XI. 186 *atri ignes* of a pyre.

27. **consiliis,** 'your deep schemes': cf. *Epist.* I. 5. 15 *potare incipiam patiarque vel inconsultus haberi.*

28. **in loco** = *in suo loco,* ἐν καιρῷ : cf. *Epist.* I. 7. 57 *properare loco et cessare et quaerere et uti.*

Ode XIII.

To Lyce, perhaps the same woman who is addressed in III. 10. She is now old but still tries to appear young and gay. See I. 25 for another poem in the same style.

Metre. Fifth Asclepiad.

1. **audivere—di, di audivere**, cf. III. 5. 18 *ego—vidi, vidi ego. vota,* 'curses.'

6. **lentum,** 'unmoved': cf. Ovid *Am.* III. 6. 60 *qui tenero lacrimas lentus in ore videt.*

virentis, in the bloom of youth: opp. to *aridas quercus,* l. 9.

7. **psallere is** properly to play the lyre with the fingers, not with the plectrum.

Chiae, a common name of freedwomen : cf. Lesbia, Delia, Barine.

8. **excubat,** 'keeps vigil': apparently imitated from Soph. *Antig.* 782 Ἔρως—ὃς ἐν μαλακαῖς παρειαῖς Νεάνιδος ἐννυχεύεις.

9. **importunus,** 'ruthless': cf. Cic. *Rep.* I. 33 *tam enim esse clemens tyrannus quam rex importunus potest.*

aridas. For the same comparison cf. I. 25. 19.

10. **luridi,** 'yellow.'

12. **capitis nives.** Quintilian (VIII. 6. 17) calls this a harsh metaphor, derived from a remote resemblance (*a longinqua similitudine ducta*).

13. **Coae purpurae,** silk gauze made in Cos.

14. **cari,** 'precious': cf. Ovid *A. A.* III. 129 *caris aures onerate lapillis.*

semel, 'once for all': as I. 24. 16.

15. **notis fastis,** archives of which the contents are well known. Everybody knows the age and antecedents of Lyce.

16. **dies,** 'time.'

17. **venus**=*venustas*, 'charm.'

decens with *motus*, 'graceful gesture': as in Quint. I. 10. 26 *corporis decens et aptus motus, qui dicitur* εὐρυθμία.

18. **illius, illius,** i.e. of the Lyce that I remember.

20. **surpuerat,** syncopated from *surripuerat*: cf. *Sat.* II. 3. 283 *unum me surpite morti.* Horace elsewhere uses *puertia* for *pueritia, divisse* for *divisisse* and *excessemus* for *excessissemus.*

21. **Cinaram,** see IV. 1. 3 *n. post* not of time, but of rank, as III. 9. 6 *neque erat Lydia post Chloen.*

dotium (see critical note). The gen. depends both on *felix* and on *nota*: cf. *Sat.* I. 9. 12 *o te, Bolane, cerebri felicem* and *C.* II. 2. 6 *notus animi paterni*: 'a face which, next after Cinara's, was famous for its happy endowment of charms.'

22. **facies,** grammatically in apposition to the subject of *spirabat* and *surpuerat.*

24. **parem,** proleptically: 'until you match the age of an old raven.'

25. **vetulae,** cf. III. 17. 13 *annosa cornix.*

26. **fervidi,** contrasted with the cold extinct ashes of Lyce's beauty.

Ode XIV.

To Augustus, on the exploits of Tiberius. This ode, and the fourth, on the exploits of Drusus, formed the nucleus of the whole book. The campaign took place B.C. 15.

Scheme. What honours, Augustus, can immortalize your services to Rome? With your soldiery Drusus conquered the Genauni, while his elder brother swept away the Rhaeti, as a torrent scours the country-side. Yours were the men, yours the strategy, yours the good fortune: for the victory happened on the very day when, fifteen years ago, Alexandria surrendered to your arms. Now all the world owns you for its master.

Metre. Alcaic.

1. **patrum—Quiritium** for the official *senatus populusque Romanus.*

2. **plenis,** 'adequate': cf. *ad plenum* 'to the full' I. 17. 15.

3. **in aevum,** 'for all time.'

4. **titulos,** inscriptions on monuments and statues: cf. IV. 8. 13 *n.* For example, later on (B.C. 2), the senate and people gave to Augustus the title *pater patriae* and decreed that it should be inscribed on his own house, in the curia and on the *quadriga* which was dedicated to him in his forum.

memores fastus, cf. III. 17. 4.

5. **qua**, over the whole space where: cf. Cic. *pro Mil.* 98 *qua fines imperii populi Romani sunt.*

habitabilis, i.e. inhabited, ἡ οἰκουμένη.

6. **principum.** For *princeps* as a title of Augustus, cf. I. 2. 50 *n.*

7. **quem—didicere—quid posses.** An imitation of the Greek usage, whereby the subject of the subordinate clause is inserted as object of the principal clause: cf Soph. *O. T.* 15 ὁρᾷς μὲν ἡμᾶς ἡλίκοι προσήμεθα and Ter. *Eun.* 656 *illum nescio qui fuerit.*

8. **Vindelici.** This seems to be used as a generic name for the various tribes Genauni, Breuni, Rhaeti.

9. **quid posses**, cf. IV. 4. 25–28 *sensere quid posset.*

10. **Genauni, Breuni,** neighbouring tribes, who occupied the valleys of the Adige and the Inn. The Brenner pass is thought to commemorate the Breuni. Among the Alpine tribes whose names were inscribed on the *tropaea Augusti* (see II. 9 *n.*) were the *Breuni, Genaunes, Vindelicorum gentes quattuor.*

13. **deiecit** is appropriate only to *arces*, but suggests *stravit* for *Genaunos Breunosque.*

plus vice simplici = 'with more than a bare requital.' For *plus* = *plus quam*, cf. Livy XXIX. 25 *parte plus dimidia rem auctam*: and for *vice* cf. Ovid *Am.* I. 6. 23 *redde vicem meritis.* Of course *vice plus simplici* is a litotes for 'with twofold punishment.'

14. **maior Neronum**, i.e. Tiberius, who advanced from the West, across the lake of Constance, while Drusus attacked from the South.

17. **spectandus—quantis fatigaret.** The Greek construction used in ll. 7–9 is here thrown into the passive. As Wickham says '*spectandus quantis* etc. implies a possible active *spectare aliquem quantis* etc.' He compares θαυμαστὸς ὅσοις. 'It was a sight to see with what fierce overthrow he wore down the courage of hearts resolute to die in freedom.'

20. **qualis.** The construction is *qualis Auster,* etc. (*tali modo*) *impiger* etc. Objection has been justly taken to *prope* as prosaic.

indomitas, 'indomitable.' (*Introd.* p. xxiv.)

21. **exercet**, 'drives.'

22. **scindente nubes**, 'shining through the torn clouds.' Orelli interprets 'breaking the clouds into showers.'

impiger vexare. *Introd.* p. xxiii.

24. **ignes** is probably to be taken literally, of burning villages. This gives some extra point to *frementem*, as if the horse snorted in fear of the flames. Many edd. however interpret *ignes* as 'the hottest of the fray.'

25. **sic**, corresponding to *ut* of l. 29. The simile is imitated from *Iliad* v. 87.

tauriformis. River-gods were generally represented as bull-headed or at least horned, either as typical of their branching streams or because of the roaring noise of mountain-torrents: cf. Eurip. *Ion* 1261 ὦ ταυρόμορφον ὄμμα Κηφισοῦ πατρός and Verg. *Georg.* IV. 371 *et gemina auratus taurino cornua vultu Eridanus.*

26. praefluit, IV. 3. 10.

Dauni Apuli, III. 30. 10.

30. ferrata, 'steel-clad,' with steel breastplates. Kiessling suggests that the Rhaeti, like the Cimbri, may have connected the front rank of their warriors with chains.

diruit, cf. *ruinis* l. 19.

32. sine clade, i.e. without loss of his own men, ' unscathed.'

34. divos, i.e. the gods who gave the favouring auspices (l. 16). The *auspicia*, on opening the campaign, were taken by Augustus himself, but he delegated the *ductus*, or actual command, of the expedition. So Suetonius (*Oct.* 21) says of Augustus *domuit—partim ductu, partim auspiciis suis—Raetiam et Vindelicos ac Salassos.*

quo die. The date of the surrender of Alexandria is Aug. 1st B.C. 30. Tiberius seems to have fought a decisive battle on the same day in B.C. 15.

35. portus. There were three harbours at Alexandria. The *vacua aula* is the palace of the Ptolemies which Cleopatra deserted (l. 37. 25).

38. reddidit, 'has given once more.'

39. peractis imperiis, 'your past campaigns' (Wickham). The following stanzas illustrate these campaigns.

40. arrogavit=*addidit*: cf. *Epist.* II. 1. 35 *chartis pretium quotus arroget annus.* The word seems to be formed, as Mr Page suggests, on the analogy of *prorogo, abrogo,* etc. and to signify properly 'to make an addition by *rogatio* or bill introduced before the people.'

41. Cantaber, cf. II. 6. 2, III. 8. 22. The Cantabri were finally conquered by Agrippa B.C. 19.

42. Medus. The Parthians surrendered the standards taken from Crassus in B.C. 20.

Indus, Scythes. Both these nations are said to have sent embassies to Augustus when he was at Tarraco B.C. 25. See on II. 9.

43. praesens, 'mighty' as I. 35. 2.

45. te is governed by *audit* l. 50.

fontium etc. refers chiefly to the Nile, but perhaps also to the Danube.

46. Nilus. The allusion is to the Aethiopians who sent an embassy to Augustus in Samos B.C. 22–21.

Hister for the Dacians (IV. 15. 21) conquered by M. Crassus B.C. 28–25.

Tigris for Armenia, whither Tiberius made an expedition B.C. 20.

47. beluosus, a new word, the meaning of which is represented in III. 27. 26 by *scatentem beluis pontum.*

48. Britannis. Augustus says, in the Monumentum Ancyranûm, that Dumnobellaunus and another British king fled to him for refuge, but the date is unknown.

49. Galliae, gen. but some MSS. have *paventes Galliae,* which would be nom. plur. and refer to the provinces of *Aquitania, Lugdunensis* and *Belgica.*

non paventis funera. The Gauls were considered to be a particularly fearless race. Lucan (I. 454) speaks of them as a people *quos ille timorum Maximus haud urget, leti metus* and Aelian calls them φιλοκινδυνότατοι.

51. Sygambri, the German people who defeated Lollius in B.C. 16 (IV. 2. 36 and IV. 9).

52. compositis, 'laid to rest.'

Ode XV.

To Augustus, a recital of the beneficent results of his rule.

Metre. Alcaic.

2. increpuit lyra, 'rebuked me with his lyre,' by striking the strings angrily: cf. Verg. *Ecl.* 6. 3 *cum canerem reges et proelia, Cynthius aurem Vellit et admonuit.*

4. vela darem. For the same metaphor of 'launching' into poetry, cf. Verg. *Georg.* II. 40–46. The expression 'not to launch my little sail upon the Tyrrhene sea' means 'not to attempt too grand themes' or *magna modis tenuare parvis.*

5. rettulit, 'has brought rich harvests' again to fields desolated by the civil war.

6. signa. The standards taken from Crassus seem to have been placed by the Parthians in some temple (cf. *Epist.* I. 18. 56 *sub duce qui templis Parthorum signa refigit*). They were surrendered to Augustus B.C. 20 and were placed by him first on the Capitol (hence *nostro Iovi*), but were afterwards removed to the *cella* of the new temple of Mars Ultor.

8. vacuum duellis. For *duellis* cf. III. 5. 38 and for the abl. Livy V. 41. 5 *viae occursu hominum vacuae.*

9. Ianum Quirini, 'the Janus of Quirinus.' The word *Ianus* here means the temple: cf. Livy I. 19 *Ianum ad infimum Argiletum indicem pacis bellique fecit.* The proper name of the god was Janus Quirinus or Geminus, and many edd. would read *Ianum Quirinum* here. Augustus closed the temple three times, in B.C. 29, B.C. 25 and B.C. 8. It had not been closed since B.C. 235.

10. frena licentiae iniecit. The reference is to the legislation of Augustus in regard to vice and luxury, e.g. the sumptuary law of B.C. 22 and the law on marriage proposed in B.C. 18.

12. artes, rules of conduct, practically 'virtues,' as in III. 3. 9.

13. Latinum nomen, i.e. the Latin race: cf. Livy III. 8. 10 *Volscum nomen prope deletum est.*

15. **porrecta** =*porrecta est,* 'was spread.'

20. **inimicat,** a word invented by Horace but borrowed from him by later poets.

21. **qui—bibunt,** cf. II. 20. 20 *Rhodani potor* and III. 10. 1.

22. **Iulia,** i.e. of Augustus.

Getae, (III. 24. 11) a neighbouring people to the Daci.

23. **Seres.** The Chinese interfered in Parthia about B.C. 28, but do not seem to have come in contact with the Romans. See on I. 12. 56, III. 29. 27.

Persae, the Parthians.

24. **Tanain—orti,** Scythians, or Cossacks of the Don.

25. **nosque,** 'and we,' to show our duty to you.

lucibus, 'days,' as IV. 11. 19.

28. **adprecati,** another invention of Horace's, used afterwards by Appuleius.

29. **virtute functos,** imitated from the common expression *vita functus* (cf. *ter aevo functus* II. 9. 13). *duces vir. functi* means 'leaders who have lived a manly life.'

more patrum (with *canemus*). Cicero (*Tusc.* I. 2, and IV. 2) cites Cato to witness that, in ancient times, the guests at a feast would sing, to the flute, songs about famous men. Augustus perhaps, who was fond of restoring old institutions, had revived this practice.

30. **remixto** =*permixto,* a sense peculiar to Horace: cf. *A. P.* 151 *sic veris falsa remiscet.*

32. **progeniem Veneris,** the Julian family.

CARMEN SAECULARE.

An ode written, by command of Augustus, to be sung in public at the *Ludi Saeculares*, a grand religious ceremony intended to celebrate the inauguration of the new régime. The proposal to hold such a celebration was first made in B.C. 23, but it was not carried out till the summer of B.C. 17. Augustus, anxious as usual to give his innovations the sanction of old tradition, revived for the occasion the *Ludi Terentini* (or *Tarentini*) which had been held in B.C. 249 and 146, and which ought, apparently, on the direction of the Sibylline books, to have been held once in every *saeculum*. The management of the revival was entrusted to the *XVviri sacris faciundis* (who had charge of the Sibylline books) with the assistance of Ateius Capito, a learned antiquarian. The scope of the ceremony was, however, greatly enlarged. The *Ludi Terentini* were a festival for the propitiation of Pluto and Proserpine, held in *Terentum*, a corner of the Campus Martius, where there seems to have been a warm spring. The *Ludi Saeculares*, however, were largely devoted to heavenly (not infernal) deities, especially Apollo and Diana.

A description of the celebration is given by Zosimus (II. 5), a historian of the 5th century, but a more authentic and exact account has been lately discovered. In Sept. 1890, during the excavations necessary for the new embankment of the Tiber, large fragments were found of an inscribed column, set up by order of Augustus as a record of the ceremonies observed at the Ludi Saeculares. The inscription (printed with notes by Mommsen in *Monumenti Antichi* 1891 p. 618 sqq.) contains a letter of Augustus to the XVviri, two decrees of the XVviri and the order of proceedings. The festival began on the night of May 31st B.C. 17 and lasted 3 nights and 3 days. Sacrifices were offered, on the 1st night to the Moirai, on the 2nd to the Ilithyiai, on the 3rd to Terra Mater (Ceres): on the 1st day (June 1st) to Juppiter on the Capitol, on the 2nd to Juno Regina, on the 3rd to Apollo and Diana. Augustus alone offered the prayers and sacrifices at night, but he was joined by Agrippa in the ceremonies of the daytime. That part of the inscription which relates to this ode belongs to the description of the proceedings on the 3rd day, and runs as follows :

sacrificioque perfecto pueri (X)XVII, quibus denuntiatum erat, patrimi et matrimi, et puellae totidem carmen cecinerunt, eo(de)mque modo in Capitolio.   Carmen composuit Q. Hor(at)ius Flaccus.

It appears therefore, that the ode was sung on the Palatine (at the temple of Apollo) and on the Capitol: but as Jupiter and Juno are nowhere expressly mentioned in the poem, Mommsen thinks the choir (27 boys and 27 girls) sang in a procession from the Palatine to the Capitol and back again.

The meaning of a *saeculum* was evidently a matter of high dispute. Horace (no doubt accepting the decision of Augustus) defines it as 110 years (see l. 21): Livy (quoted by Censorinus *c.* 17) gave it as 100 years: the Emperor Claudius, thinking Augustus wrong, held the Ludi again in A.D. 47: and Domitian, disagreeing with Claudius, held them in A.D. 88, when Tacitus himself was one of the XVviri (see *Ann.* XI. 11). Many further details are given in Smith's *Dict. of Antiquities*, 3rd ed. s.v. *Ludi Saeculares*, but the column above mentioned was discovered after the date of the article.

Scheme. Phoebus and Diana, hear our prayers. O Sun, maintain the pre-eminence of Rome. Ilithyia, protect our nursing mothers and give long life to their offspring. Ye Fates, let our good fortune in the future be equal to the past. Earth, grant us bounteous harvests. Hear, O Apollo, the boys: Diana, hearken to the girls. If, by your aid, Aeneas came to Italy, prosper now our land with all goodness and happiness, and grant the prayers now offered by Caesar, who has vanquished every nation and restored every virtue. Apollo hears and answers: Diana inclines her ear to our entreaty: yea, all the gods accord us their favour.

Many attempts have been made to apportion the stanzas between the two choruses of boys and girls: but in this matter nothing can be considered certain except that ll. 33, 34 were sung by the boys and 35, 36 by the girls. It would seem that Horace, when he wrote the ode, was imperfectly acquainted with the order of proceedings, for, though he mentions the Fates, Ilithyia and Tellus (i.e. the deities who were worshipped at the nocturnal ceremonies), he does not mention Jupiter and Juno, to whom one day each was granted. (See also note to l. 14.)   The last stanza seems to have been added as some compensation for the omission.   The last but one, also, seems to have been added at a time when it was proposed that the procession should go from the Palatine to the Aventine (Diana's temple) and not from the Palatine to the Capitol.   If this be so, we might imagine that the ode at first contained 17 stanzas, of which the first 8 were sung by both choruses, the 9th was divided and the last 8 again were sung by both.

1. **silvarum potens.**   For the gen. cf. *diva potens Cypri* I. 3. 1, and for the attribute of Diana cf. I. 21. 5, III. 22. 1.

2. **decus.**   For the sing. referring to two deities, cf. *clarum Tyndaridae sidus* IV. 8. 31.

5. **Sibyllini versus,** not the original Sibylline books (which were burnt in the fire on the Capitol B.C. 82) but a collection of Sibylline

prophecies made in B.C. 76 to replace the books. Augustus, after sifting these and rejecting many as spurious, deposited the remainder in the temple of Apollo on the Palatine. They seem to have been all written in Greek hexameters. (See *Sibyllini libri* in Smith's *Dict. of Antiq.* 3rd Ed.) The Sibylline verses on which the ritual of the *Ludi Saec.* was founded, are given by Zosimus (as above cited). They begin as follows:

> Ἀλλ' ὁπόταν μήκιστος ἵκῃ χρόνος ἀνθρώποισι
> Ζωῆς, εἰς ἐτέων ἑκατὸν δέκα κύκλον ὁδεύων,
> Μέμνησ', ὦ 'Ρωμαῖε, καὶ οὐ μάλα λήσεαι αὐτῶν
> Μεμνῆσθαι τάδε πάντα κ.τ.λ.

If these lines are genuine, it seems strange that there should have been any dispute as to the duration of a *saeculum*.

6. virgines lectas etc. There were 27 girls and 27 boys. This number (*ter noveni*) appears to have been usual in Roman choruses: Livy XXVII. 37 and XXXI. 12.

lectas—castos. Each epithet belongs to both boys and girls (cf. III. 4. 18, 19). They were to be children of parents religiously married (*confarreati*). of patrician or at least senatorial rank, and *patrimi et matrimi* (i.e. having both parents living, ἀμφιθαλεῖς).

7. septem colles. The original *Septimontium* was confined to certain spots on the Palatine, Esquiline and Caelian. By the *septem colles* Horace doubtless means the whole city, including the Capitol, Palatine, Aventine, Caelian, Esquiline, Viminal and Quirinal.

9. alme sol etc. Wickham suggests that the connexion between the description and the prayer is 'Unchangeable yourself, though you cause change and seem to change, give to the pre-eminence of Rome the same unchangeableness.'

13. rite. 'Thou whose kind office it is to bring children to birth in due time.' *rite*='after thine office' (Wickham): cf. *Aen.* III. 36 *nymphas venerabar agrestes...rite secundarent visus. aperire partus* seems to mean 'to make the way easy for births.' For *lenis aperire* cf. *non lenis recludere* I. 24. 17 and *Introd.* p. xxiii.

14. Ilithyia. The goddess of birth, identified by the Greeks with Artemis. Horace seems to identify her with Diana, who again was sometimes identified with Juno Lucina: thus Catullus (34. 13) addresses Diana as *tu Lucina dolentibus Iuno dicta puerperis*. In the ceremonies of the Ludi Saeculares, however, sacrifice was offered on the second night to the *Ilithyiai*. (Both the inscription cited in the Introd. and Zosimus have the plural: the latter calls them κυανέας Εἰλειθυίας.) These were two goddesses, daughters of Juno and in no way connected with Diana. Horace apparently did not consult the XVviri before writing.

16. Genitalis. This title, whether of Juno or Diana, is not found elsewhere, nor is there any Greek title exactly corresponding. To be known by many names conferred glory on a divinity; and Artemis, in a hymn of Callimachus, expressly asks Zeus to give her πολυωνυμίη: cf. *Sat.*

11. **6.** 20 *Matutine pater seu Iane libentius audis*, Aesch. *Prom.* 209 ἐμοὶ
δὲ μήτηρ...Θέμις καὶ Γαῖα, πολλῶν ὀνομάτων μορφὴ μία.

17. **producas**, 'rear' to mature years: cf. 11. 13. 3.

18. **patrum decreta.** The allusion is to the *Lex Iulia de mari-
tandis ordinibus*, which was sanctioned by a senatus consultum, but
rejected by the comitia, in B.C. 18. It was carried later, but when, and
with what alterations, cannot be determined. It imposed penalties on
celibacy and gave rewards to the parents of a numerous progeny.

19. **prolis feraci**, cf. *fertilis frugum* l. 29.

20. **lege marita**, cf. *maritum foedus* Ovid *ex P.* III. 1. 23.

21. **per annos**, 'every 110 years,' as *per autumnos* 'every autumn'
11. 14. 5. The estimation of the *saeculum* at 110 years is given in the
Sibylline verses (see *Introductory Note*).

22. **orbis**, 'cycle,' κύκλος in the Sibylline verses.

referatque. For the position of the verb cf. *pedes tetigitque crura*
11. 19. 32.

24. **frequentis**, emphatic, 'attended by a mighty throng.' Of
course, if the population diminished, the *ludi* could not be *frequentes*.

25. **veraces cecinisse**: in effect, 'you who have always prophesied
the truth, prophesy now good fortune equal to the past.'

Parcae, the Fates, Μοῖραι, to whom sacrifice was offered by
Augustus on the first night of the festival : cf. *Parca non mendax*
11. 16. 38.

26. **quod semel dictum** etc., 'that which, once pronounced, an
immovable landmark preserves for ever.' For *semel* 'once for all' cf.
I. 24. 16, I. 28. 16 etc. For *terminus* cf. *Aen.* IV. 614 *et sic fata Iovis
poscunt, hic terminus haeret.* For the subj. *servet* cf. I. 32. 2, 3 *si quid
—Lusimus tecum quod et hunc in annum Vivat.* For *per aevum*
Bentley quotes, among many other passages, Lucr. I. 549 *servata per
aevum.* The ordinary reading *quod semel dictum est stabilisque rerum
Terminus servet* is generally interpreted: 'As once and for aye has been
promised—and may Time's irremovable landmark protect the promise!'
as if *quod semel dictum est* anticipated *bona fata* and *Terminus servet*
were a prayer. But it is unlikely that Horace left *cecinisse* without an
object or that he allowed the cacophony of *dictumst stabilisque*, and
rerum terminus is almost incomprehensible. Moreover, if the Parcae
are *veraces* and the fate has been pronounced once for all, it seems
useless to add the special prayer *terminus servet*.

27. **peractis**, sc. *fatis*; cf. IV. 14. 39.

29. **Tellus** was worshipped on the third night of the *ludi*.

30. **spicea—corona.** The reference is to the Ambarvalia, a rustic
festival held at the time when the sickle was first put into the harvest.
The ears of corn first cut were made into a garland for the image of
Ceres. See Tibullus II. 1.

31. **salubres** and *Iovis* both belong to *aquae* and *aurae*. See on
lectas—castos l. 6.

33. **telo,** the arrows which caused pestilence, as described in the first book of the Iliad.

35. **bicornis,** wearing the crescent.

37. **Roma—opus.** In the Trojan war, Apollo and Artemis were on the side of the Trojans and between them saved the life of Aeneas: for when he was wounded, Apollo extricated him from the fight and Artemis healed his wound (*Il.* v. 443–448). At the fall of Troy, Apollo begged for the preservation of Aeneas (IV. 6. 21–26) and commanded him to sail to Italy (*Aeneid* IV. 345).

For *si* in adjurations cf. I. 32. 1, III. 18. 5 and *infra* l. 65.

38. **litus Etruscum,** i.e. the shore of the *mare Etruscum* or Tyrrhene sea: as I. 2. 14.

39. **pars,** in apposition with *turmae. iussa* is emphatic: 'the remnant that *you* commanded.'

41. **sine fraude,** 'unscathed,' as II. 19. 19.

42. **castus,** emphatic, explaining why Aeneas was so favoured.

43. **munivit,** 'paved a free path.' *munire viam* is properly to build a highroad.

44. **plura relictis,** 'more than they left behind.'

45. **di,** Apollo and Diana chiefly are addressed.

47. **Romulae genti,** IV. 5. 1.

prolemque. For the hypermetric syllable cf. IV. 2. 22, 23 and *Introd.* pp. xxvi, xxix.

49. **quaeque,** accus. with *veneratur*: 'those things which he asks of you with prayer and sacrifice': cf. *Sat.* II. 6. 8 *si veneror stultus nihil horum.*

50. **clarus—sanguis,** i.e. Augustus, descendant of Iulus.

51. **bellante prior,** cf. *Aen.* VI. 854 *parcere subiectis et debellare superbos.*

54. **Albanas securis,** i.e. the Roman fasces. Alba Longa was the mother-city of Rome. For *secures* cf. III. 2. 19.

55. **Scythae, Indi.** See IV. 14. 42 *n.*

57. **Fides et Pax** etc. All the deities who departed after the golden age are now returning. *Honos* and *Virtus* had adjoining shrines: see Livy XXVII. 25. 7.

60. **cornu,** abl. with *beata*: 'rich with full horn': cf. I. 17. 16.

61. **augur,** I. 2. 32.

62. **acceptus**=*gratus.* The term is usually applied to a gift, in the formula *gratum acceptumque.*

63. **salutari arte.** The allusion is to another aspect of Apollo, that of the Healer, Παιάν, the father of Asklepios.

65. **si**='so surely as he regards with favour his altar on the Palatine.' This is the same use of *si* that we had in l. 35: meaning 'if it be true that,' and implying that it is true.

66. **felix** probably applies equally to *rem Rom.* and *Latium*: 'prolongs the prosperity of the Roman empire and Latium.' But *felix* may be masculine and apply to Apollo (= 'benign'): cf. Verg. *Ecl.* 5. 65 *sis bonus o felixque tuis.*

67. **lustrum**, i.e. the cycle of 110 years. So Martial (IV. 1. 7), referring to the celebration of the Ludi Saec. by Domitian, says *hic colat ingenti redeuntia saecula lustro, Et quae Romuleus sacra Terentus habet.* Most edd. however think that *lustrum* here is only 5 years and that Horace alludes to the renewal (in B. C. 17) of Augustus's *imperium proconsulare* for five years. But the period is absurdly short and, besides, Augustus held the *tribunicia potestas* (which was as important as the *imperium*) for life.

68. **prorogat.** The poet speaks with assurance on behalf of Apollo. The reading *proroget* is well supported, but we have had prayers enough: cf. l. 74.

69. **Aventinum Algidumque.** Two very ancient shrines of Diana, the former founded by the Latin league, the latter by the Aequians.

70. **quindecim virorum,** i.e. the *X Vviri sacris faciundis* who had charge of the Sibylline books and the surveillance of any new rites. Augustus himself and Agrippa were both members of the college.

71. **puerorum,** 'children,' the boys and girls of the chorus.

73. **sentire.** The word is often used (like *sententiam dare*) of voting in the senate. Juppiter and all the gods in council vote with Apollo and Diana.

75. **doctus,** taught by Horace, who was χοροδιδάσκαλος.

CONSPECTUS METRORUM.

I. Archilochīum primum :

  − ⏑͡⏑ − ⏑͡⏑ −, ⏑͡⏑ − ⏑͡⏑ − ⏑ ⏑ − ⏝   hexam. dact.

  − ⏑ ⏑ − ⏑ ⏑ ⏒   Archilochīus minor.

  IV 7.

II. Asclepiadēum primum :

  − − − ⏑ ⏑ −, − ⏑ ⏑ − ⏑ ⏒   versus Asclepiadēus

  IV 8.   minor.

III. Asclepiadēum secundum sive maius :

  − − − ⏑ ⏑ −, − ⏑ ⏑ −, − ⏑ ⏑ − ⏑ ⏒ versus Asclepi-

  IV 10.   adēus maior.

IV. Asclepiadēum tertium :

  − − − ⏑ ⏑ − ⏑ ⏒   versus Glyconēus.

  − − − ⏑ ⏑ −, − ⏑ ⏑ − ⏑ ⏒ v. Asclepiadēus minor.

  IV 1. 3.

V. Asclepiadēum quartum :

  − − − ⏑ ⏑ −, − ⏑ ⏑ − ⏑ ⏒ v. Asclepiadēus minor.

  − − − ⏑ ⏑ −, − ⏑ ⏑ − ⏑ ⏒   ,,

  − − − ⏑ ⏑ −, − ⏑ ⏑ − ⏑ ⏒   ,,

  − − − ⏑ ⏑ − ⏑ ⏒   v. Glyconēus.

  IV 5. 12.

VI. Asclepiadēum quintum :

— — — ⏑ ⏑ — , — ⏑ ⏑ — ⏑ ⏒   v. Asclepiadēus minor.

— — — ⏑ ⏑ — , — ⏑ ⏑ — ⏑ ⏒   „   „

— — — ⏑ ⏑ — ◡̄   v. Pherecratēus secun-
                                             dus acatal.

— — — ⏑ ⏑ — ⏑ ⏒   v. Glyconēus.

IV 13.

VII. Sapphicum minus :

— ⏑ — — — , ⏑ ⏑ — ⏑ — ◡̄   versus Sapphicus minor
                                                hendecasyllabus.

— ⏑ — — — , ⏑ ⏑ — ⏑ — ◡̄   „   „

— ⏑ — — — , ⏑ ⏑ — ⏑ — ◡̄   „   „

— ⏑ ⏑ — ◡̄   v. Adonius.

IV. 2. 6. 11. carm. saec.

VIII. Alcaicum metrum :

◡̄ — ⏑ — — , — ⏑ ⏑ — ⏑ ⏒   v. Alcaicus hendeca-
                                                syllabus.

◡̄ — ⏑ — — , — ⏑ ⏑ — ⏑ ⏒   „   „

◡̄ — ⏑ — — — ⏑ — ◡̄   v. Alcaicus enneasyl-
                                             labus.

— ⏑ ⏑ — ⏑ ⏑ — ⏑ — ◡̄   v. Alcaicus decasyl·
                                             labus.

IV 4. 9. 14. 15.

Printed in the United States
By Bookmasters